Julia Rubio

Upcycling Books

Decorative Objects

SCHIFFER
PUBLISHING

4880 Lower Valley Road · Atglen, PA 19310

Other Schiffer Books on Related Subjects:

An Introduction to Calligraphy, Véronique Sabard, Vincent Geneslay, and Laurent Rébéna; foreword by Roger Druet; photos by Laurent Geneslay, ISBN 978-0-7643-5230-0

Beginning Illumination: Learning the Ancient Art, Step by Step, Claire Travers, ISBN 978-0-7643-5027-6

Copyright © 2019 by Schiffer Publishing, Ltd.

Originally published as *Upcycling Books: Objetos Decorativos* by Parramon Paidotribo, S.L., Spain © 2017 Parramón Paidotribo
Translated from the Spanish by Ian Hayden Jones

Library of Congress Control Number: 2019936480

Cover design by Jack Chappell
Editorial direction: María Fernanda Canal
Editor: Esther Serra
Text and handicraft exercises: Julia Rubio
Graphic design: Josep Guasch
Page layout: Estudi Guasch, S. L.
Photography: Nos & Soto
Type set in WiesbadenSwing/Univers 55

ISBN: 978-0-7643-5875-3
Printed in China

Published by Schiffer Publishing, Ltd.
4880 Lower Valley Road
Atglen, PA 19310
Phone: (610) 593-1777; Fax: (610) 593-2002
E-mail: Info@schifferbooks.com
Web: www.schifferbooks.com

For our complete selection of fine books on this and related subjects, please visit our website at www.schifferbooks.com. You may also write for a free catalog.

Schiffer Publishing's titles are available at special discounts for bulk purchases for sales promotions or premiums. Special editions, including personalized covers, corporate imprints, and excerpts, can be created in large quantities for special needs. For more information, contact the publisher.

We are always looking for people to write books on new and related subjects. If you have an idea for a book, please contact us at proposals@schifferbooks.com.

How to access additional material
VIA THE WEB PAGE

Go to **books2ar.com/upy** and click on the LOGIN link. Then enter the following:

Email: SchifferPublishing
Password: UB_2019

TYPES OF ADDITIONAL CONTENT:
Look for these symbols with the project:

VIDEO

TEMPLATE

Template. Print and view templates.

Video. Shows a process or technique in detail.

Contents

Het was de eerste schooldag in Obaba. De nieuwe onderwijzeres
liep van bank naar bank met de leerlingenlijst in haar hand. 'En
jij? Hoe heet jij?' vroeg ze toen ze bij mij was aangekomen. 'José,'
antwoordde ik, 'maar iedereen noemt me Joseba.' 'Goed zo.' De
onderwijzeres wendde zich tot de jongen naast mij in de bank, de
laatste aan wie ze haar vraag nog moest stellen: 'En jij? Wat is
jouw naam?' De jongen deed mijn manier van antwoorden na: 'Ik
ben David, maar iedereen noemt me de zoon van de accordeo-
nist.' Onze klasgenoten, jongens en meisjes van een jaar of acht,
negen, grinnikten om zijn antwoord. 'O ja? Is je vader accordeo-
nist?' David knikte. 'Ik ben dol op muziek,' zei de onderwijzeres.
'We zullen je vader eens naar school halen om een concertje te
geven.' Ze leek opgetogen, alsof ze net een bijzonder verheugend
bericht had ontvangen. 'David kan ook accordeon spelen. Hij is
een kunstenaar,' zei ik. De onderwijzeres keek verrast: 'Echt
waar?' David ___ me ___ por ___ zij ___ elle ___ og zz, eg ___ wa u,' be
___ ___ de ik. En b ___ ___ heet ___ ___ a ___ ordee ___ bij ___.

Intro
duction

Upcycling Books: For the love of books!

As bookworms we derive a pleasure far beyond the simple act of reading. The buzz starts as we plan a purchase, selecting a title in advance—before we head out to the bookstore, before we even have a copy in our hands. Once at the store we carefully open and smell the stiff new pages. Finally we head home to bury our noses in it on rainy days and quiet nights. Later we will remember its characters and lines or passages that stand out; sometimes we will base important decisions on the things it has taught us. But what happens when a book is old or damaged and no longer in a fit state to read?

Books must endure house moves and holidays . . . we lend them to our friends and they are passed from reader to reader. They may be tattered, or outdated, but we still can't bring ourselves to throw them away. Wouldn't it be better to give them a new lease on life, a new purpose and significance, rather than leave them to gather dust on a shelf?

This volume presents more than 20 decorative projects ideal for book lovers and DIY and upcycling enthusiasts, using recycled pages and covers from your favorite books. These projects require a minimum of effort and use simple techniques and inexpensive materials. Supplementary templates, videos, and variations will further stimulate your creativity. *Upcycling Books* will inspire the "crafties" among us to reclaim their favorite passages, fill their homes with the aroma of an old library, and live a more sustainable lifestyle.

Long live books!

Tools and Materials

THE GOLDEN RULE of upcycling is to reuse as many different materials as possible, meaning that the first phase of any new project involves scouring our homes for any items and tools that we may already have on hand. With some improvisation, everyday household objects can serve the same purpose as the tools that we suggest you use (e.g., a unused CD could be used to trace a circle in place of a compass, or you could recycle an old photo frame instead of buying one from a junk dealer).

Books

We will focus on books that are damaged, obsolete or have simply seen better days. If you find that you don't have the required materials at home, you could always visit secondhand shops, book fairs, flea markets, or the antique bazaars that are becoming commonplace in cities all over the world.

Each and every part of a book can be recycled, from a solitary page to the entire text block and the spine, cover, and dust jacket. Obviously, what can be created with our books depends largely on their condition.

We can empty a book to make a flower tray or jewelry box. We can festoon a lampshade with garlands made from a handful of carefully sculpted pages. If we remove the text blocks from smaller books they can form the sides of a birdhouse. If we can rescue only the spine, it can be used as part of a secret storage box or magazine rack. A cover is easily transformed into a case for electronic devices, a mail organizer, or a jewelry box.

Cutting Tools

Depending on the book's condition remove the text block's endleaves or carefully and patiently tear pages out by hand. Nevertheless, cutting tools are indispensable for most book upcycling projects.

Scissors are your basic go-to tools when cutting up recycled pages. While there are many different types, office and kitchen scissors are best suited for this task. For those who may be scrapbooking enthusiasts, there are different finishing effects that can be produced by using scalloped **craft scissors**, although they are by no means essential.

To remove a book's entire text block or cut strips of paper with straight edges you will need a very sharp, handheld **paper cutter (scalpel)**. It's a good idea to use a **cutting board** so that you do not damage the surface you are working on. An **aluminum ruler** will help make your edges crisper and more precise.

Drawing Tools

Mark out the areas that you will cut on pages or paperboard with a **regular pencil**. If the surface you wish to cut is dark in color you could use **white pencil, crayon, or chalk**, any traces of which can be easily and completely removed. Use **permanent felt-tip pens** to mark plastic or laminated surfaces, although you will not be able to delete these marks later on.

Piercing Tools

Manual punches that cut paper to different shapes are very useful when upcycling. They are inexpensive and time-saving. They can punch one or several pages at a time, producing identical shapes and avoiding the repeated use of templates.

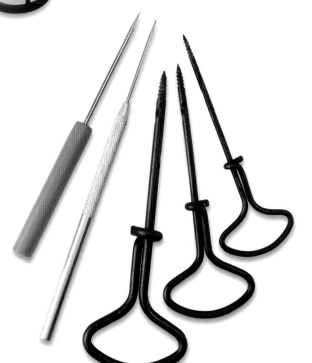

Use a **gimlet** to make holes in hardback covers, wooden boards, and hardboard, as it allows you to manually and delicately pierce finer materials which may prove difficult with a handheld electric drill. A **scalpel**'s sharp blade is especially useful for making precise incisions and trimming book covers.

Joining Tools

Solvents and adhesives will bind your upcycled components together and make them more robust. But it is **paint and sealant** that make a finished article more durable, readying them for everyday use. You will need different sized paintbrushes to apply glue, paint, and sealant.

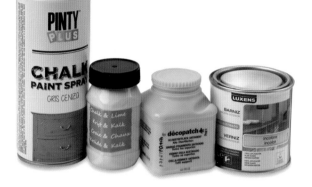

In addition to their age-old use of sewing fabrics, **thread and string** can also be used to join together paper and add finishing touches to your projects.

Glue and paste bind fragile book materials firmly together, preparing them for everyday use. Use a variety of clips, pins, and clamps to hold the different components in place while they dry.

THIS MANUAL AIMS to inspire new upcycling ideas and the creation of everyday objects, rather than achieving the perfect finish. It does not demand a high level of skill; we simply explain how attractive objects can be made using the most basic handicraft techniques, with materials that can be found in every home. Above all, you will learn how to solve any problems that may arise as you work to complete these projects using the materials you have on hand.

Techniques

Cutting Techniques

We use the same, simple and easy cutting techniques with some variation depending on which part of a book we wish to recycle.

To make **straight or precise cuts** to create strips or paper shapes, use a scalpel guided by an aluminum rule. Be careful to apply only a small amount of pressure and make repeated passes over the material, rather than trying to cut right through with a single stroke.

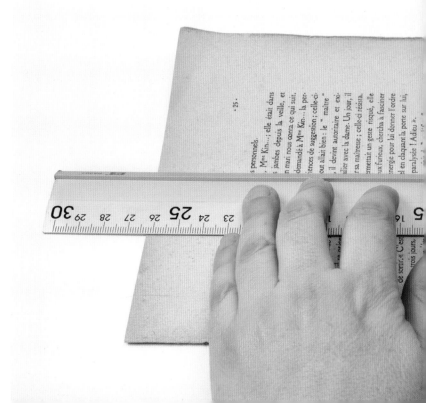

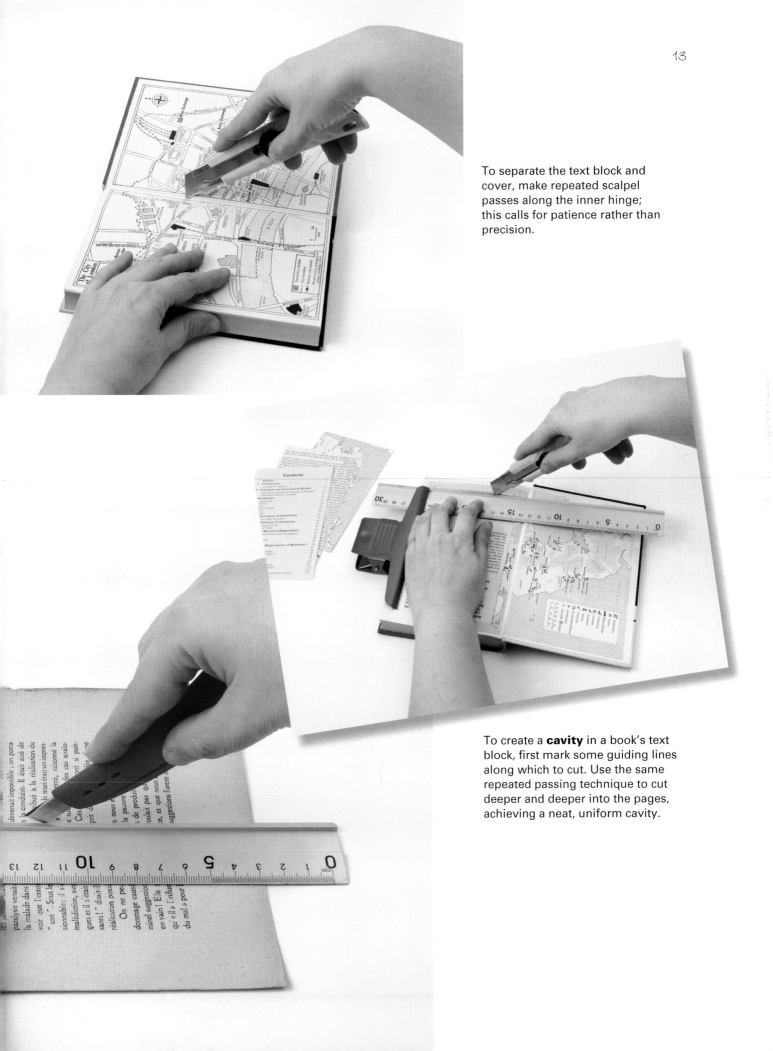

To separate the text block and cover, make repeated scalpel passes along the inner hinge; this calls for patience rather than precision.

To create a **cavity** in a book's text block, first mark some guiding lines along which to cut. Use the same repeated passing technique to cut deeper and deeper into the pages, achieving a neat, uniform cavity.

Use straight-edged scissors to **cut** recycled pages into strips of paper. Use scalloped craft scissors to give your strips jagged edges.

Reduction is the best technique to employ when you want to make small incisions in a hardback cover.

Mark a point before **piercing** a book cover, rotating your gimlet like a drill.

Paper-Working Techniques

There are many different **paper-working techniques**, ranging from basic to advanced. This book uses the simplest techniques, producing impressive and robust three-dimensional upcycling projects.

It may seem like child's play, but **rolling paper strips** is useful for making smaller components. Once they are glued in place they can be combined with other elements, enhancing any project with a higher level of detail.

Pages can be folded manually, similar to origami. Or you can mark out or score folding lines with a bone paper folder or the blunt edge of a cutting tool.

Overlapping or **braiding** strips of folded paper uses a traditional crafting technique similar to basket weaving. This creates sturdier and longer-lasting decorative objects.

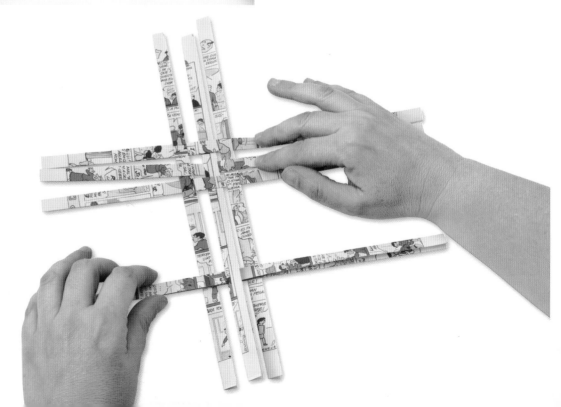

Joining Techniques

Each new project requires a combination of joining techniques to attach or bind its components in place. These techniques will simultaneously protect your upcycling and make it more resilient.

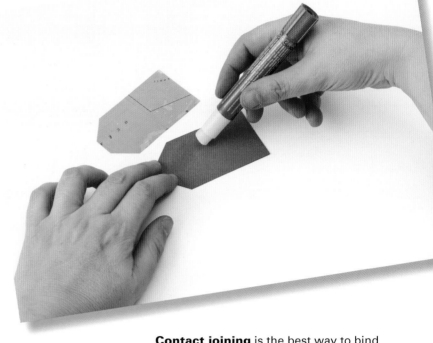

Contact joining is the best way to bind paper together and reinforce cardboard templates. Simply apply a thin, even layer of glue between surfaces.

Basic sewing techniques can also be used to join components together and add an attractive finish. It will also make your upcycling projects sturdier.

Use a brush to **spread glue** across the sides of a text block. As it dries it will stick the pages together and serve as an invisible, protective sealant.

Sealant is key to a better finish, protecting your upcycling output and making it sturdier.

Lining pages with plastic adhesive film is a great way to make them more durable, preparing the object for everyday use.

DIY

Projects

YOU CAN BREATHE NEW LIFE into the tattered old pages of our favorite books
by creating decorative objects inspired by classic literary themes. With just a few pages or
a cover and a little imagination you can create vases, smartphone chargers, photo frames,
lampshades, wall hooks, or secret storage boxes to keep our important documents safe. You
can also learn how to build a clock, keeping half an eye on the time as you wile away the
hours with our favorite novels and perhaps even dream of writing our own. You never know!

Party Ideas

Decorating for a party or special event can be a stimulating and creative process. With a few damaged pages and a spark of inspiration you can produce decorations for any celebration. Garlands are easy to make and offer great variety; you can fashion flower or heart shapes, form chains from strips or circles of paper, etc. No child's party would be complete without paper windmills to delight the little ones. There are as many items to create as there are reasons to hold a party in the first place! Let's look at some of them.

1. For each flower you need: Two tattered old book pages, scissors, nylon thread, clear (transparent) glue, bulldog clips to hold the pages in place, and a manual punch to crop paper shapes.

2. Shape the long sides of both pages with the manual punch. If your punch can cut through two pieces of paper at a time then the design on the side of each page will be the same.

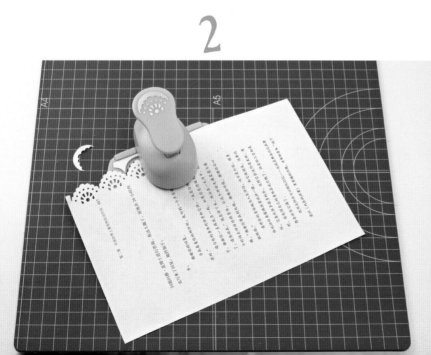

3. Fold the pages in on themselves, forming two small "accordions." These folds must be regular and equal to the height of the punch shapes.

4. Once you have pleated the pages, **fold** them in half. Put them together and join them with the nylon thread. Secure them with a knot.

5. Gently **open** the accordion folds and join the edge of one page to another. Repeat this procedure with the other edges.

Once the edges have been stuck together, tease open the folds to improve your flower's structure and appearance.

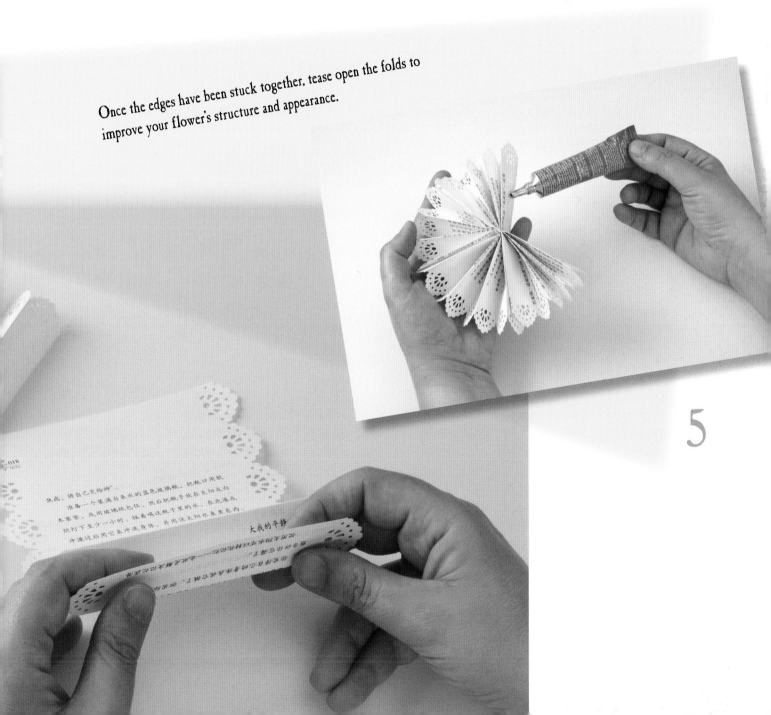

5

6. Hold the edges of the pages together with bulldog clips until the **glue dries**. You can join several flowers to form a garland, or simply decorate with single flowers.

6

Your paper flowers are now ready to brighten up any celebration. All that's left to do is attach them to the ceiling and walls at different heights to enhance that festive mood!

Variations

Paper garlands made from circles are simple decorations to create. Just cut equally sized circular shapes from old book pages and glue them together along a colored piece of string.

Make **decorative windmills** from a square piece of paper. Cut along all four vertices and fold in the corners, then use a pin to attach the corners to a wooden shaft. You can fashion a simple chain consisting of looped or heart-shaped paper strips to form a garland.

A recycled **glass jar** can become an improvised light source, brightening up any celebration. You can make a novelty candleholder by attaching a strip of paper punched with star shapes to your jar, then tying off the neck with a ribbon.

Purse

If your favorite comic has seen better days, you can transform its pages into something fresh and unique. A purse is not only a practical accessory but also the perfect way to recycle old, damaged, full-color pages that you might not want to throw away because of their sentimental value. You can even fold your new purse in half so that it fits inside your pocket while you go shopping for other comics to add to your collection.

1. **You will need:** Some dog-eared pages from old comics, a scalpel, scalloped craft scissors, a ruler, plastic adhesive film, permanent marker pen, a bone paper folder, cutting board, needle and thread, a gimlet, and a self-adhesive velcro patch.

2. Prepare two different-sized sheets of paper, using a scalpel and the ruler as a guide to **remove** their white borders. Cut one of them to a third of the size of the other (this will become your purse's separator).

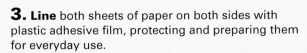

3. Line both sheets of paper on both sides with plastic adhesive film, protecting and preparing them for everyday use.

4. Score two fold lines onto the larger of the two sheets using a bone paper folder. The goal is to fold the sheet into three equal sections, just like a commercial letter.

5. Place both sheets together, aligning the smaller sheet within the central folded section on the larger sheet. Mark out $\frac{3}{8}$ in. (1 cm) intervals with the permanent marker and rule.

6. Pierce the paper at each $\frac{3}{8}$ in. (1 cm) interval mark with a gimlet. Be sure to use a cutting board to protect your working surface.

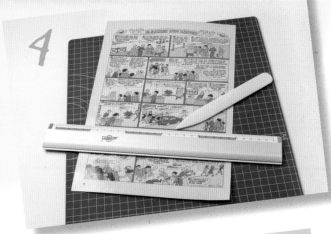

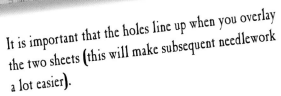

It is important that the holes line up when you overlay the two sheets (this will make subsequent needlework a lot easier).

7

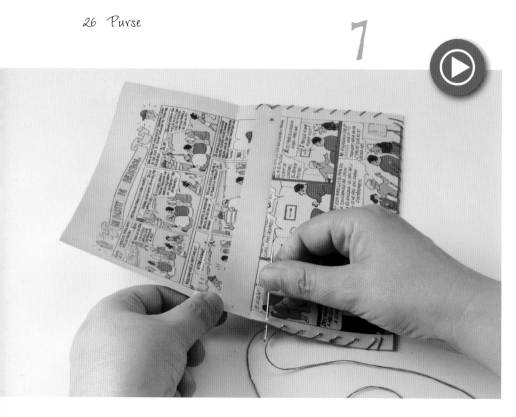

7. Correctly align the two sheets (with the smaller sheet "sandwiched" within the central folded section of the large sheet) and then hand-sew them together. Thread the needle through the holes first one way and then the other, creating a decorative stitching effect.

After you have finished sewing, tie off the ends of the thread with a discreet knot. Trim the upper section of your purse with the scalloped craft scissors for a nicer finish.

Stick two halves of the velcro patch in place at the center of your purse, so that they make contact once the flap (upper section) is closed.

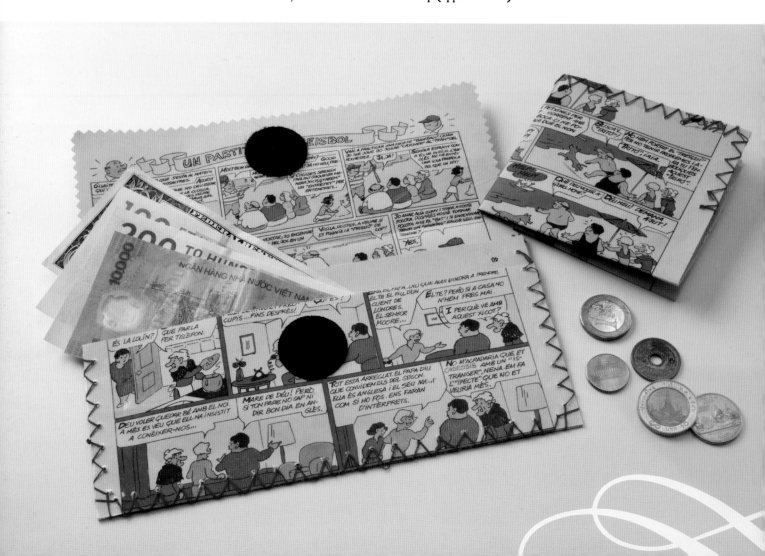

Variations

You can also employ the same concept to add a personal touch to gift wrap. In this illustration you can see how a circular bookbinder has been used to close our gift wrapping at one end. You can add variety to our finished gift wrap by using the pages of older or distinctly different books.

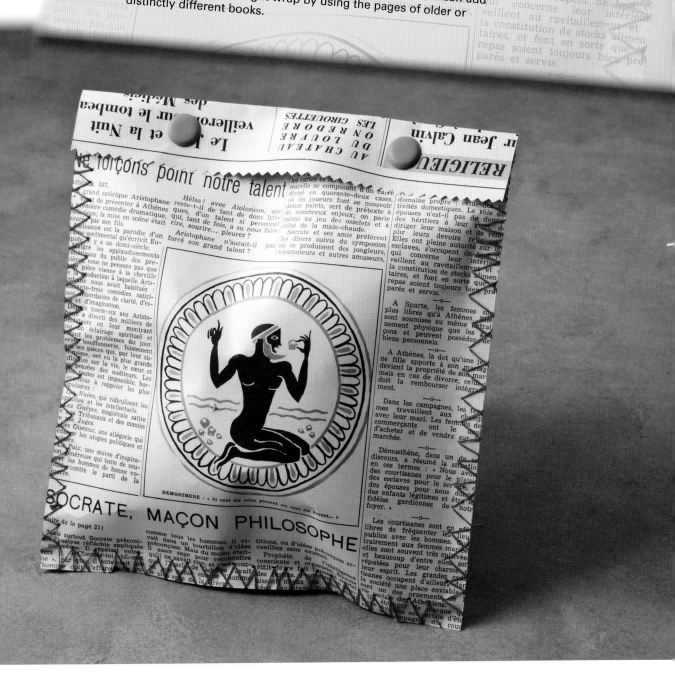

The purse is now ready to carry your notes and coins! If you prefer a more compact purse that will fit into your pocket, score it vertically and fold it in half (taking care not to displace the velcro patch). You can create a cardholder by adding more separators.

You can make hanging mobiles of all shapes and sizes from the pages of a book. Children will be thrilled to see their bedrooms decorated with their favorite themes: birds, butterflies . . . a mobile will pique their curiosity and capture their imagination. Older children will enjoy going out to the woods to gather twigs as well as helping to bring your design to life.

Child's Bedroom Mobile

1. You will need: A battered old book, cardboard sheets, a pencil, adhesive tape, scissors, a few twigs, a paintbrush, chalk paint, nylon thread, a glue stick, and sandpaper (optional).

2. We will make a mobile with 10 paper birds (although you can use as many as you like) that will liven up the corner of any room. First download the template and then **draw out** 20 bird shapes on book pages, then 10 more on cardboard.

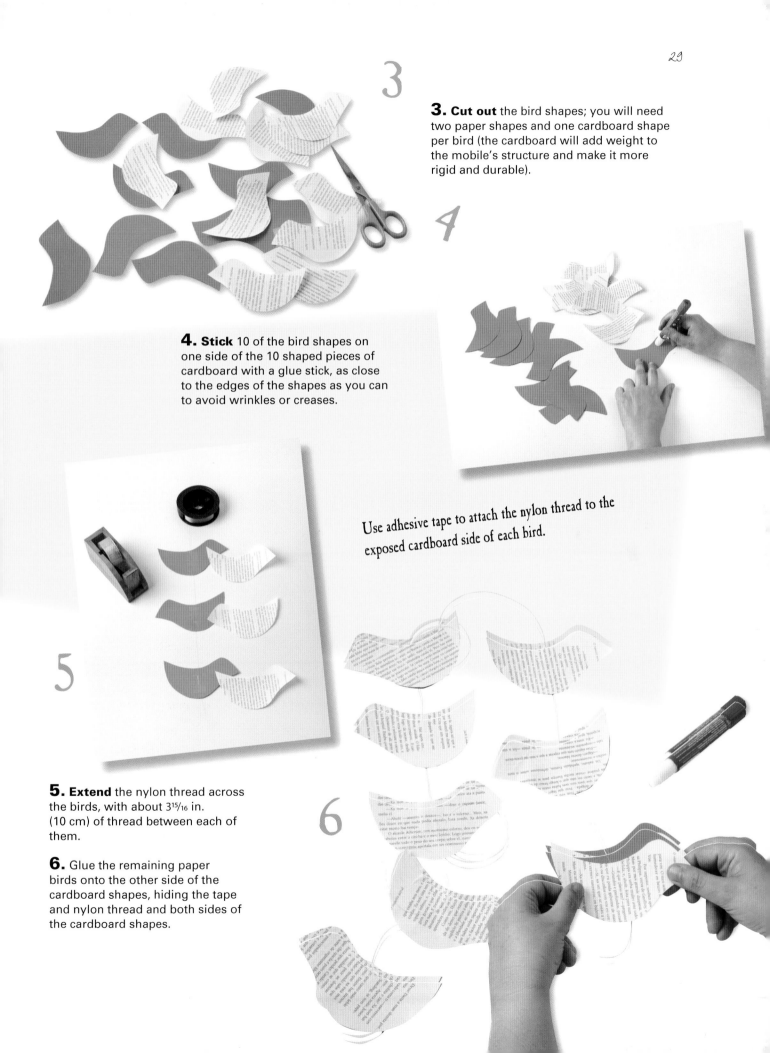

3. Cut out the bird shapes; you will need two paper shapes and one cardboard shape per bird (the cardboard will add weight to the mobile's structure and make it more rigid and durable).

4. Stick 10 of the bird shapes on one side of the 10 shaped pieces of cardboard with a glue stick, as close to the edges of the shapes as you can to avoid wrinkles or creases.

Use adhesive tape to attach the nylon thread to the exposed cardboard side of each bird.

5. Extend the nylon thread across the birds, with about 3¹⁵/₁₆ in. (10 cm) of thread between each of them.

6. Glue the remaining paper birds onto the other side of the cardboard shapes, hiding the tape and nylon thread and both sides of the cardboard shapes.

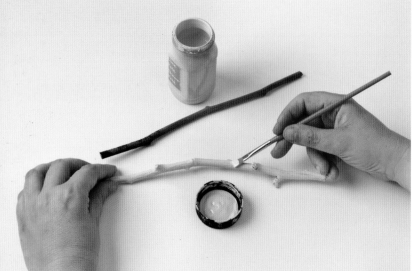

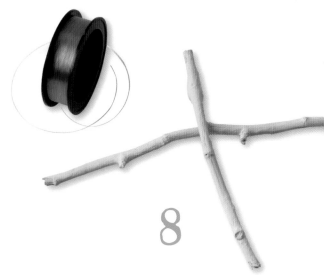

7. Two wooden sticks (rods or thin twigs) of about 9¹³⁄₁₆ in. (25 cm) in length will form our hanging cross section. Twigs should be cleaned; any knots and blemishes can be removed with **sandpaper** before use. Apply the chalk paint with a brush, concealing imperfections in the wood (this may require a second coat).

8. Form a **crosspiece** by tying the sticks together in the center with nylon thread. Tie another length of thread around the center so that you can later hang your mobile from the ceiling. Working on a flat surface, tie your cardboard shapes to the end of each stick. Try and distribute weight equally to balance the mobile; here we have interspersed sections (two sections with three birds attached and two sections with two birds attached).

Variations

Another way to create attractive mobiles from recycled books is to use a wooden embroidery frame as a hanging section (you can hang as many threads from the circle as you want). Here you can see butterfly shapes created with a small manual punch, while the larger butterflies have been cut out with scissors. Attaching them directly to the nylon thread with adhesive tape gives the mobile a delicate visual effect.

We have **simply and effectively** transformed the pages of a damaged book into a decorative object. It's easy to combine different shapes along different lengths of thread depending on where you plan to hang your mobile.

We often need to recharge our smartphone's battery. For this project you will create a retro-style charger cradle, associating this daily task with the pleasure of reading. You only need a few basic tools and two unused books. The main cable will be hidden within the cradle, leaving our smartphone to rest on a decorative base.

Smartphone Charger

1. You will need: Two unused hardback books, graphite pencil, white pencil, a rule, scalpel, PVA adhesive glue, a paintbrush, and a few bulldog clips.

2. Measure the book with a rule to identify its midpoint and then draw a cross with your white pencil (as book covers are normally a dark color) about 13/16 in. (2 cm) distance from the spine.

1

2

3

4

3. Use the scalpel to score a small rectangle over the cross. **Pierce** the cover carefully, slicing through its layers of cardboard one by one until you have cut a neat rectangular hole.

4. Use the rectangular hole in the cover to mark where you will cut into the text block. Open the book to its endleaves and draw two parallel lines about ³⁄₁₆ in. (0.5 cm) apart, from the mark you have made to the very edge of the text block.

5

A rule helps us to cut straight and true.

5. Cut into the text block right along the length of the two parallel lines.

6

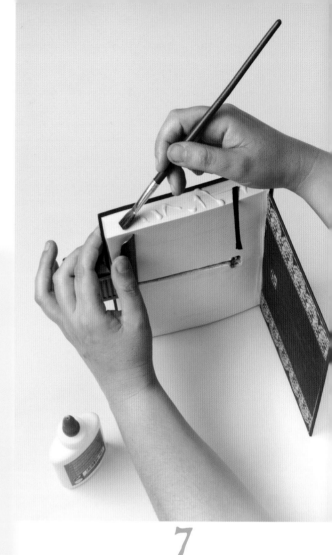

6. Create a **notch** by making repeated cuts along the two lines, until you have cut through the entire text block.

7. Hold the text block firmly in place with bulldog clips, then spread PVA adhesive **glue** around its three sides. Be careful not to get any glue on the cover, which you will need to open and close when installing your charger.

8. Leave the text block clamped together until the glue dries, ensuring that it remains closed and compact.

7

8

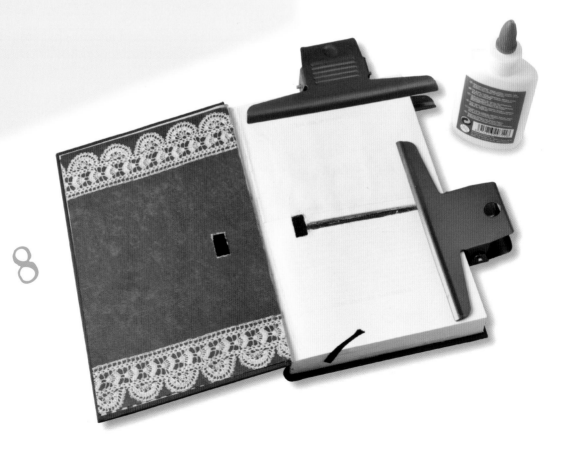

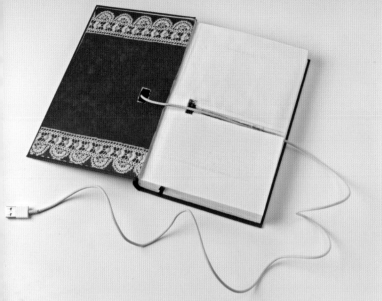

9

9. Once the text block is dry, **install** the charger by running its cable along the notch that you have cut. Pass the charger's head (plug) through the hole you have made in the cover. This is where your smartphone will stand.

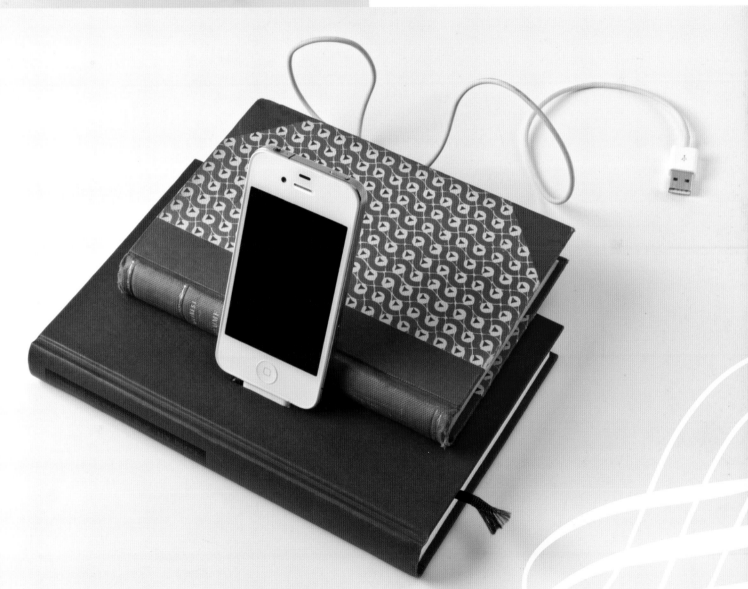

Our charger is almost ready! All you need to do is place another book on top of the first book. This will help to support our smartphone (you can add further stability by gluing the second book in place).

Woven Basket

This woven basket recycles the pages of an old atlas and will keep small objects such as buttons and pencils safe. It can be placed on any flat surface and makes an excellent sewing box, keeping your different threads, etc., organized and close at hand. Whatever you decide to use it for, this upcycling project will teach you a basic braiding technique.

1

1. You will need: A number of pages from an old or obsolete atlas, a rule, pencil, scalpel, cutting board, transparent adhesive tape, scissors, sealant, and a paintbrush.

2. Place the pages on your cutting board, then **measure** and **cut out** 20 $1\frac{3}{16}$ in. (3 cm) wide strips to the height of the pages. Fourteen of these strips will form the framework of our basket while the other six will be woven into the sides.

2

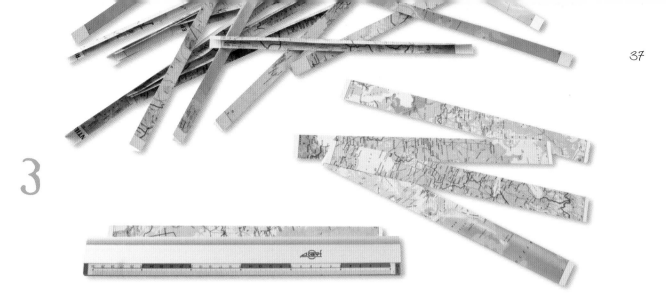

3

3. Fold each paper strip in half lengthwise along the edge of a rule, creating 9/16 in. (1.5 cm) wide strips.

4. First **weave** together six strips that will form the framework of your basket, three in each direction to form a lattice of perpendicular strips. To make this easier, leave a gap of just over 3/8 in. (1 cm) between each strip. They can be pushed together later on.

5. Add further strips one by one, weaving them into the framework until it is complete with seven strips both horizontally and vertically.

6. Once your framework is ready, **fold** the loose ends of the paper strips upwards to 90°, forming a basket shape.

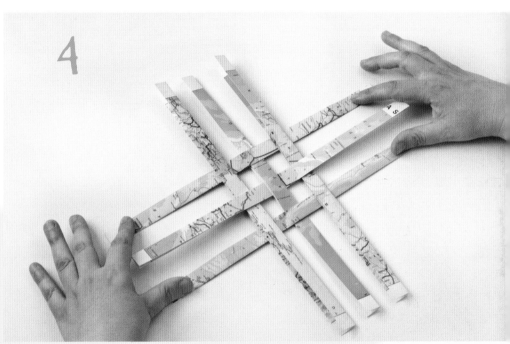

4

Push the strips together to eliminate any remaining gaps. Your framework should be bunched up as tightly as possible.

5

6

7

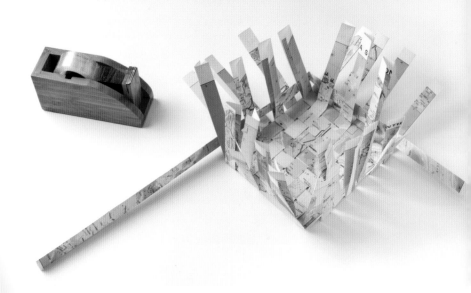

7. Make three strips double the length of the strips that you used for the framework by **taping** them end to end. Weave them in horizontally, forming the sides of your basket.

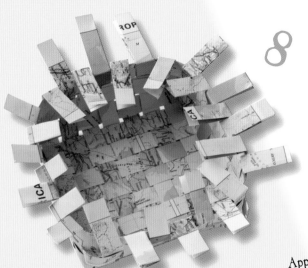

8

8. Once these three long strips are in place, **fold** the ends of any protruding strips over in opposite directions (i.e., one outward and then one inward).

9. To finish the upper part of your basket, weave any protruding strips into the framework, hiding the loose ends and reinforcing its structure.

Apply a coat of transparent sealant over the entire basket for a better finish and increased durability.

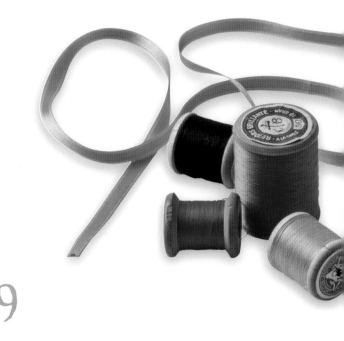

9

Variations

You can also use the weaving technique (with a generous coating of sealant) to create placemats or coasters from old newspapers and magazines.

Your basket is now ready to safeguard everyday objects! You can make several different-sized baskets, depending on what you intend to use them for.

Photo Frame with Flower Borders

Battered old book pages are perfect for creating three-dimensional pieces such as small paper flowers that you can use to decorate any part of your home. This project requires a simple cardboard scrapbooking frame, or an old unused frame (so that not only the photo you use but the frame itself will evoke memories).

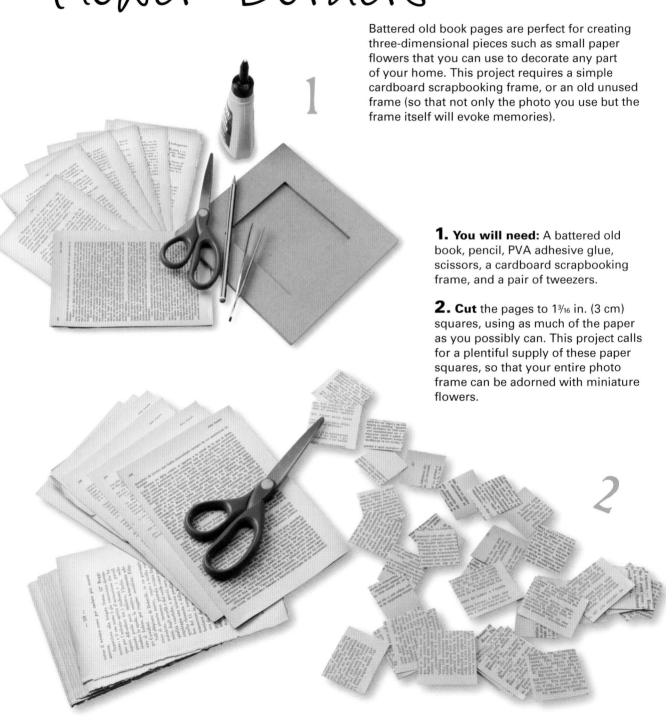

1. You will need: A battered old book, pencil, PVA adhesive glue, scissors, a cardboard scrapbooking frame, and a pair of tweezers.

2. Cut the pages to 1³⁄₁₆ in. (3 cm) squares, using as much of the paper as you possibly can. This project calls for a plentiful supply of these paper squares, so that your entire photo frame can be adorned with miniature flowers.

3

3. Cut circles out of your paper squares. Note that they don't have to be perfect!

Use a compass to mark out the circles first, if you find it easier.

4

4. Draw spirals on each circle with your pencil. Locate its point in the center of a circle before spiraling evenly out, until you reach the circle's edge.

5

5. Next **cut along** the spiral pencil lines. Your paper circle will assume a "corkscrew" shape.

Starting in one corner, begin to cover the frame with flowers.

6. Take one end of the corkscrew shape and **roll it up**, forming a tiny flower. Fasten its ends with a drop of PVA adhesive glue.

7. Glue the base of your flower to the photo frame.

8

8. Continue to cover the frame, flower by flower. Stick them as closely together as possible, so that they hold each other in place as the glue dries.

9. Little by little, cover the frame entirely with flowers. Using pages that have yellowed over time (as shown here) will give your frame a "chunky," vintage feel.

9

10. Make sure that there are no gaps between your flowers, which should be tightly bunched together. If this isn't the case, **fill in** any gaps with more flowers. A pair of tweezers will make this job much easier.

Your photo frame with flower borders is finished and ready for your favorite photograph. An old, black-and-white family portrait completes the vintage effect, while a modern photograph creates a striking contrast in style.

Using small bunches of flowers will create a minimalist effect. Jewelry beads glued in the center of each flower breathe new life into any old frame.

You can make any number of shapes out of paper. Try using **smaller paper rolls** to border your frame, fixing them one by one, side by side with PVA adhesive glue.

Flowers created from paper sheets are multipurpose decorations. Attach them to polystyrene with universal transparent glue, fastening them in place with a plastic-headed pin. If you string them along a nylon thread, you create a **hanging ornament**.

Case for Electronic Devices

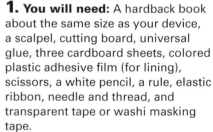

1

We are surrounded by electronic devices: Smartphones, tablets, e-books, etc., which we often carry with us in our pockets or bags. We can use the cover of an old book to give them a makeover and protect them from the rigors of everyday use, creating a delightful juxtaposition between our favorite classic authors and modern technology.

1. You will need: A hardback book about the same size as your device, a scalpel, cutting board, universal glue, three cardboard sheets, colored plastic adhesive film (for lining), scissors, a white pencil, a rule, elastic ribbon, needle and thread, and transparent tape or washi masking tape.

2

2. Open up the book and use a scalpel to **separate** the text block from the cover.

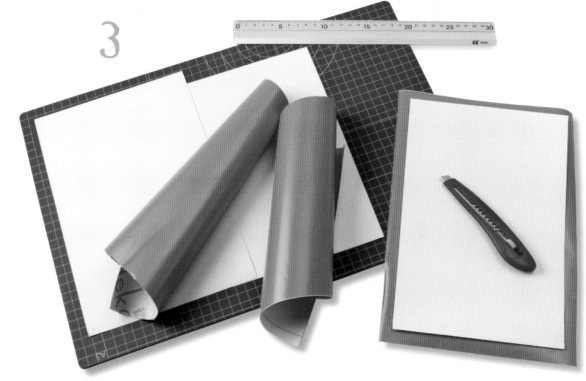

3. Cut three cardboard rectangles to the same size as the text block. **Line** them with plastic adhesive film (select a color that will complement the cover of your book), leaving a ¹³/₁₆ in. (2 cm) border around the sides. This will make the inside of your case more durable.

4. Trim off any excess adhesive film, ensuring a neat finish for your cardboard pieces and concealing any damage to the inside covers. Put the lined cardboard **to one side**, for now.

5. Measure out and mark two points at the top and bottom of the cover with a white pencil and a rule.

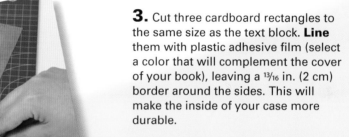

These marks should correspond to the two slots through which you will pass the elastic ribbon that secures our cover.

6

6. Cut two slots at the points you have marked to the same width as the elastic ribbon (approximately ³⁄₈ in. [1 cm]).

7. Pass the elastic ribbon through the slots. Use a needle and thread to **sew** the ends together on the inside cover.

The elastic must be taut so that your device is held firmly in place and does not move around during transit.

7

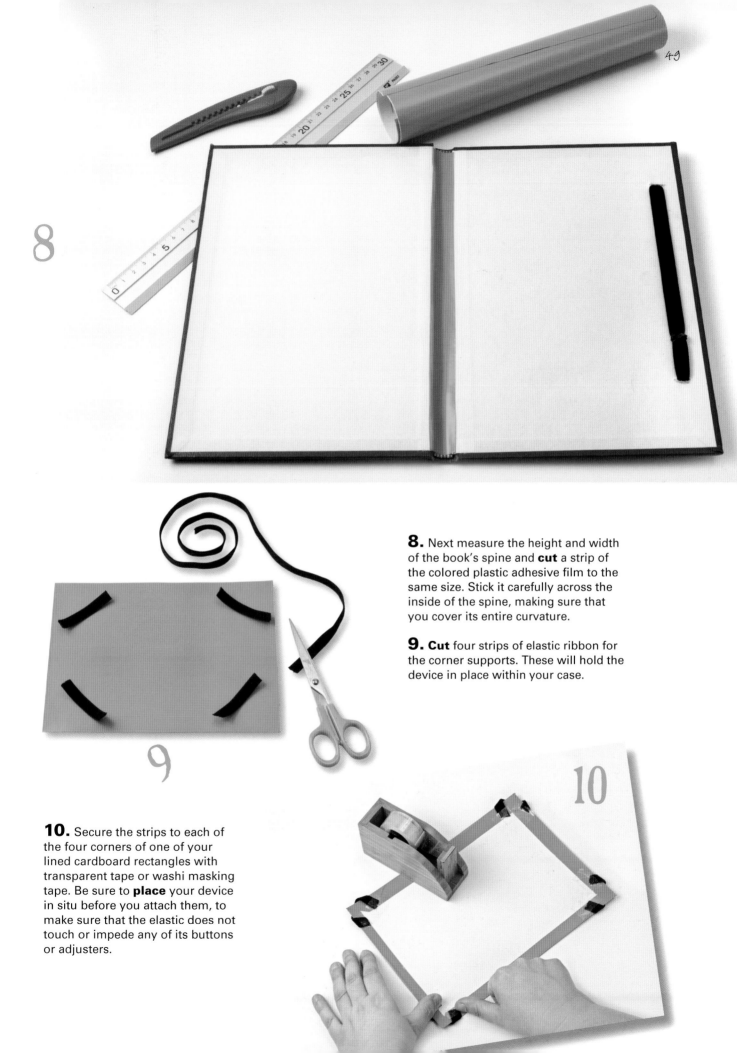

8

8. Next measure the height and width of the book's spine and **cut** a strip of the colored plastic adhesive film to the same size. Stick it carefully across the inside of the spine, making sure that you cover its entire curvature.

9. **Cut** four strips of elastic ribbon for the corner supports. These will hold the device in place within your case.

9

10

10. Secure the strips to each of the four corners of one of your lined cardboard rectangles with transparent tape or washi masking tape. Be sure to **place** your device in situ before you attach them, to make sure that the elastic does not touch or impede any of its buttons or adjusters.

11

11. Then glue the lined cardboard sheet with the elastic corner supports in place on the inside of the book's back cover (right-hand side). Place a heavy object on top to make sure that it is held in place while it dries.

Our electronic device case is now ready to carry with us wherever we go! A fitting tribute to our childhood reference books and a great way to teach an old book new tricks.

Variations

You can make a **smartphone cover with a contemporary touch** using the cover from an old, linen-bound book (here you can see how we have created a "designer notepad" effect). Upcycling is a great way to preserve artisan traditions such as bookmaking.

Line the interior of your cover with adhesive imitation leather to make it more robust. The smartphone is held in place with adhesive velcro patches.

You can create a decorative effect by using a vintage-style book cover to **protect an e-reader**, reminding us of our favorite classic reads. Again you can use self-adhesive velcro patches (attached to both the back of our eBook and the case itself) to hold it securely in place.

Jewelry Box

A tattered hardback book can be transformed into an elegant jewelry or accessory box. It's also an ideal place in which to empty the contents of our pockets at the end of the day: Coins, hairclips, travel cards, etc.

1. You will need: A hardback book, pencil, a rule, scalpel, chalk paint, PVA adhesive glue, two brushes (one to apply your glue, and the other to paint with), and removable adhesive transparent tape.

2. Carefully **cut** along the inner hinge with a scalpel. Remove the very first page of the book, exposing the first endleaf.

1

2

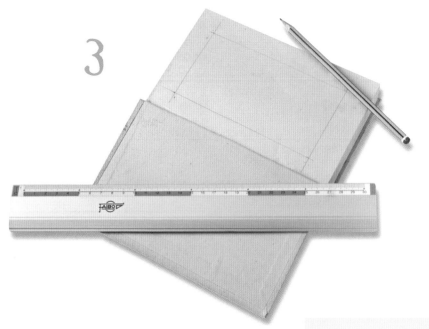

3. Draw a rectangle in pencil on the endleaf, leaving a margin of $^{13}/_{16}$ in.–1 in. (2–2.5 cm) to the edges of the text block. This will guide you later as you create a cavity.

4. Use one of your paintbrushes to **apply the glue** along the edges of the text block. Make sure that the front cover can open and close (this will become the lid of your box).

Place a heavy object on top of the book while the glue dries.

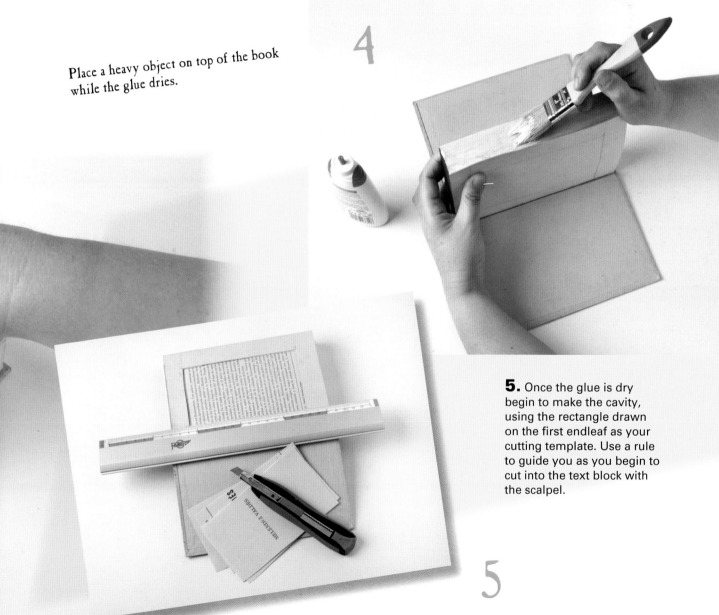

5. Once the glue is dry begin to make the cavity, using the rectangle drawn on the first endleaf as your cutting template. Use a rule to guide you as you begin to cut into the text block with the scalpel.

6. Remove the text block pages a few at a time. This is a delicate task that requires patience and great care!

7. Continue to remove pages until your box is at the required depth. If you decide to remove all of the text block pages, be careful not to cut into the back cover.

Trim away any excess paper edges from the inside of your box, leaving the sides as smooth and uniform as possible.

8. Once you have finished making the cavity, **choose** a page to decorate the bottom of your jewelry box. Here we have chosen to use the colophon.

9. Cover the spine with removable adhesive transparent tape **before the final gluing and painting** stages. This will ensure that the spine remains clean and free of paint, and your box will also retain some of the book's original character.

10

10. Apply PVA adhesive glue to the inner sides of your box (several coats will ensure that your box is more durable) and **leave it to dry** overnight.

11. Once your jewelry box is dry it is ready for decoration. Start by applying the chalk paint to its interior before moving on to the exterior.

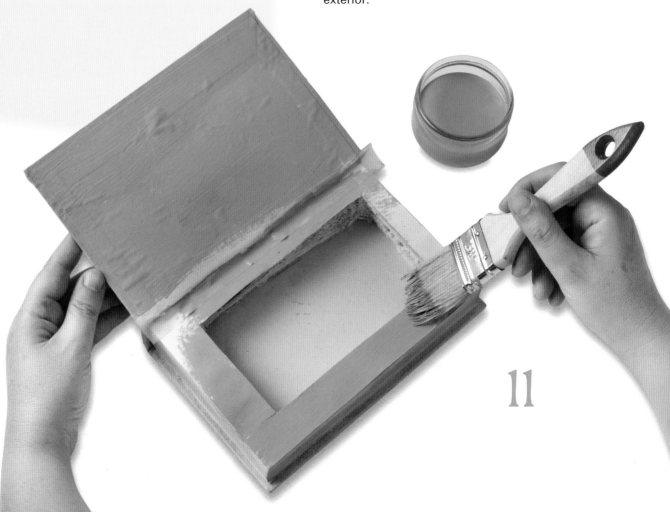

11

12. Finish off by removing the adhesive tape, revealing the unpainted spine. Glue the selected colophon to the inside back cover and cover it with a fine coat of PVA adhesive glue that will act as a transparent sealant once it is dry.

Your jewelry box is ready to safeguard your accessories and other treasures such as coins or keys that weigh down your pockets. From now on they will be both organized and easy to find, in an eye-catching box.

Retro Desk Organizer

While a desk organizer is an essential, practical addition to any home or office, there is no reason why it can't be a charming, decorative object. Here you will make a holder to keep your pens and pencils which blends retro nostalgia with contemporary style. It is cheap and easy to make, requires only a bare minimum of materials, and is a spectacular, eye-catching centerpiece for any working surface!

1. You will need: A complete or almost complete book (as this upcycling project requires plenty of pages), an empty food tin, scissors, a compass, a hot-melt glue gun and silicone refill sticks, and an old CD (optional).

2. Open the book at the center of its text block and **tear out** the pages one by one carefully, so as not to rip them. You will need at least 60 complete pages for this project.

3. Use your compass to **measure** the height of the empty food tin. You will use this measurement later as the diameter of the paper circles that will give your desk organizer its volume and shape.

4. Use your compass to **mark out** the first circle on one of the torn-out pages.

5. Alternatively, you can trace around the circumference of an **old CD** (excellent for making circles the same height as a standard food tin).

It is important to be as accurate as possible; all of your circles must be the same size.

Keep a number of extra pages on hand, just in case you need them.

6

6. Use scissors to carefully **cut out your circles**. Their edges should be smooth and free of any noticeable angles, ensuring a consistent finish.

7. You will need at least **60 of these circles** to cover a standard-sized food tin.

7

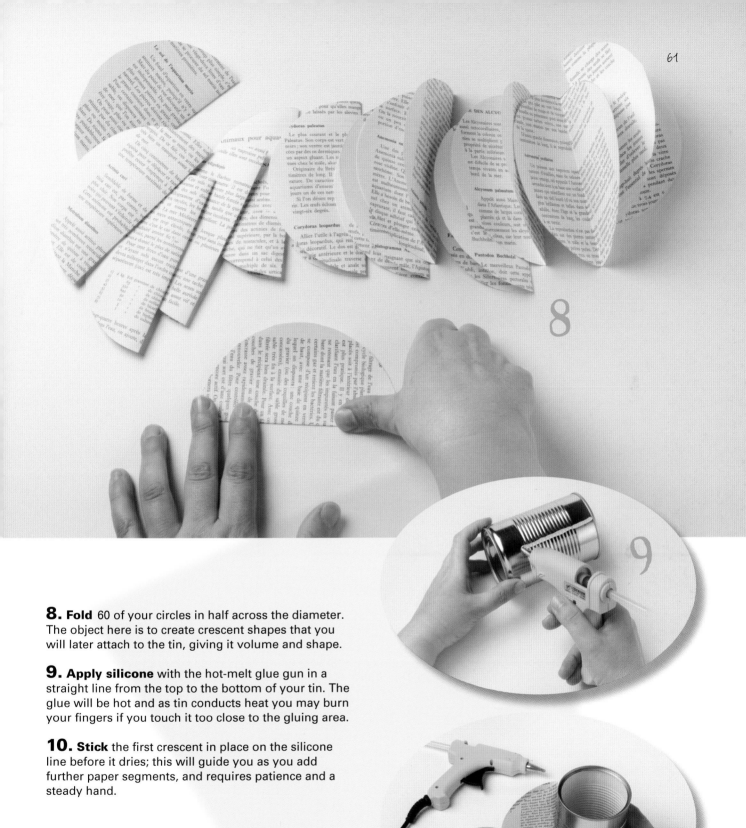

8. Fold 60 of your circles in half across the diameter. The object here is to create crescent shapes that you will later attach to the tin, giving it volume and shape.

9. Apply silicone with the hot-melt glue gun in a straight line from the top to the bottom of your tin. The glue will be hot and as tin conducts heat you may burn your fingers if you touch it too close to the gluing area.

10. Stick the first crescent in place on the silicone line before it dries; this will guide you as you add further paper segments, and requires patience and a steady hand.

12

11

11. Add successive glue lines, sticking a paper crescent to each of them. Pay close attention the direction and alignment of the text to achieve an optimal finish.

12. When you **stick the last crescent** in place, make sure that it covers the last exposed section of the tin; however, you can always reshape the paper crescents if there are any gaps.

13. Now is the time to carefully **trim off** any edges with your scissors, ensuring a consistent finish.

13

Your desk organizer is ready to fill up with pens and other writing tools, as well as cheer up your working space.

Flower Tray

A flowerpot may not be the first thing that springs to mind when upcycling an old book, but the end result is certainly eye-catching. Cacti and succulent plants (also known as "succulents") are best suited to this flower tray as they require little water to survive. This is an original decorative object that can be fitted out in any number of ways: You can use a single plant, combine different species or create a literary terrarium. The only limit is your imagination!

1. You will need: An unused book, a pencil, rule, scalpel, PVA adhesive glue, a paintbrush, bulldog clips, a plastic shopping bag, scissors, cacti and/or succulent plants, soil, and small stones for decoration.

1

2. Use your paintbrush to **spread the glue** across all three sides of the text block then glue both the front and back covers to the text block. The book is now a compact, single unit and ready for the next upcycling step.

2

3

3. It is important that the glue dries completely before you begin to form a cavity.

Use the bulldog clips so that the book retains its shape as the PVA adhesive glue dries.

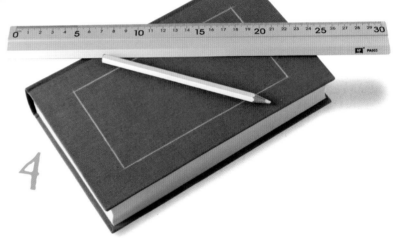

4. Draw a rectangle on the front cover of the book with pencil and rule. You might find it easier to use a white pencil, as you will need a clear guide when you begin cutting.

5. Gradually **cut away** the cover and text block with your scalpel.

4

5

6

6. The goal here is to create a cavity in the center of the book. Use your scalpel to remove a few pages at a time for clean, effective cutting. Don't cut into the last few pages.

7. Apply PVA adhesive glue to reinforce the inner sides of your flower tray; this will ensure that the interior of the text block is also stuck securely in place. You can weigh it down with a heavy object while it dries.

7

8

8. Cut a section out of the plastic shopping bag. Use this to **line** the inside of the tray. This will protect the book from the soil and plant roots, as well as the water you will use to feed your plants.

9. Attach the plastic lining to the inside of the book with PVA adhesive glue.

9

Lightly press the lining to the sides and bottom of the tray so that it sticks in place.

10

10. Now it's time to position your plants. It will help if you think about their distribution and the visual effect that you would like to accomplish beforehand.

11. Trim away any excess plastic lining with a pair of scissors. It is important to leave the lining in place while positioning the plants as this will keep the book clean.

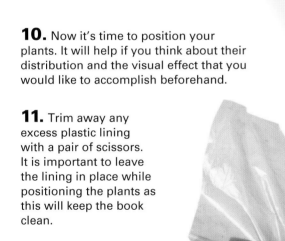

11

12. Place small stones on the soil and in between the plants, decorating and adding the finishing touches to your tray. Scissors can be used as tweezers to set the stones in place.

Your flower tray is ready for springtime, or indeed any other time of the year. You can observe how the plants grow, their roots descending into the space that was once occupied by a book's pages!

Variations

Cut a **circular cavity** into the center of the text block to make a flower tray for a single potted plant. Cacti require very little soil in which to grow and complement all kinds of decorative features.

With a little imagination you can create a terrarium inside a book. Use the same cavity-making process and then **re-create** your favorite scene from the book with toys or other small objects that you find lying around at home.

Wall Clock

Time will definitely fly with this clock hanging on your wall! The image you select is all-important for this project. The cover of a twentieth-century pulp novel replaces the humdrum circular clock face with a vivid splash of color. Just add a simple clock mechanism to create an up-to-the-minute decorative timepiece. It's also a great excuse to frequent your local flea markets as you search for books that will inspire your upcycling projects.

1. You will need: A hardback book, gimlet, scalpel, permanent marker pen, bulldog clips, a paintbrush, PVA adhesive glue, a metal wall mount, a screw, screwdriver, two circular self-adhesive velcro patches, and a battery-powered clock mechanism.

2. First of all, **select** the best point on the book's cover to mount and center your clock mechanism. The clock's hands will not lay flush to the flat surface of the book, so try to consider the overall graphic aesthetic as a three-dimensional sculpture.

3. Place the gimlet over the selected point and slowly **push it through** the cover, making sure that it doesn't pierce the text block.

4. Open the book up and secure the text block with your bulldog clips, ensuring that it remains closed and compact before spreading PVA adhesive across its sides.

5. Once the text block has dried, **apply** a generous coating of glue over the inside back cover.

6. Draw around the outline of the clock mechanism with a permanent marker on the first endleaf. This is where we will make the cavity that holds the mechanism.

The text block and back cover should be a solid, single unit after gluing.

We will use the metal wall mount to hang our clock.

7. Use your scalpel to cut a **cavity**, gradually and patiently slicing into the text block. The depth of the cavity should be the same depth as your clock mechanism.

8. Spread **glue** around the inside edges of the cavity, sticking the pages together. Screw the wall mount in place near to the top of the back cover.

9

10

9. Place the clock mechanism within the cavity then close the front cover to ensure that it is a good fit.

10. Once the mechanism is properly installed, fix the hands to the threaded pin and then secure them in place with the washer and cog.

11

11. Fasten the front cover in place with the two circular self-adhesive velcro patches, as you will need to open the book occasionally to adjust the time or change the battery. The velcro will also help to hold the mechanism in place when you hang your clock.

The clock is now ready to hang on the wall, so that you can watch the hours fly by in the most stylish way possible!

Variations

You can find inspiration in the **cover of an old adventure book**. You can paint the hands to highlight them, affix stones or plastic baubles to indicate the hours and even add scrapbook corner protectors.

A cover decorated with detail is perfect for making a clock, although the book's title will not be visible. Be sure to get a smaller clock mechanism if you are working with a smaller book!

Using the same cavity-creating technique it is also possible to **install the hands along a book's spine**. Attach books on either side to complete the effect.

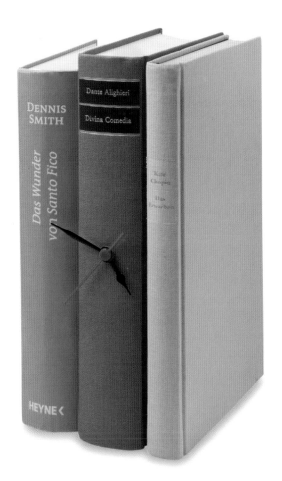

With a few simple components and using a simple Chinese lantern-making technique, you can create a Nordic-design-inspired lampshade. There are as many possibilities as shapes that the pages can be cut into; here we have cut rounded edges to make fruit-like shapes, reminiscent of artichoke leaves or pine cones.

1

1. You will need: Pages from a battered old book, a round Chinese paper lampshade, a cardboard template in the shape of a flower petal (triangular with rounded edges), rectangular metal lampshade support and ceiling hook, a pencil, scissors, universal transparent glue, and a cereal bowl.

Ceiling Lampshade

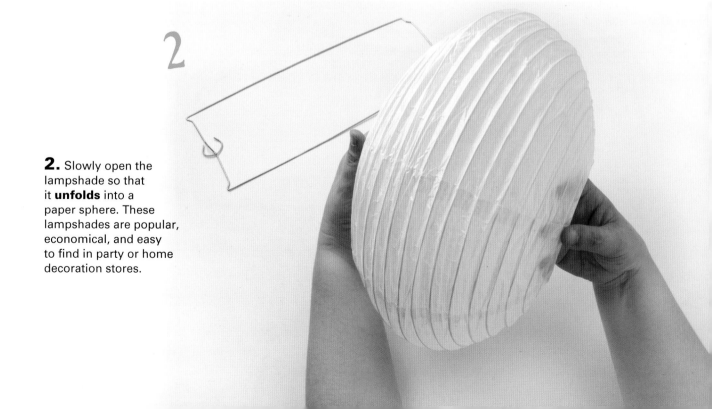

2

2. Slowly open the lampshade so that it **unfolds** into a paper sphere. These lampshades are popular, economical, and easy to find in party or home decoration stores.

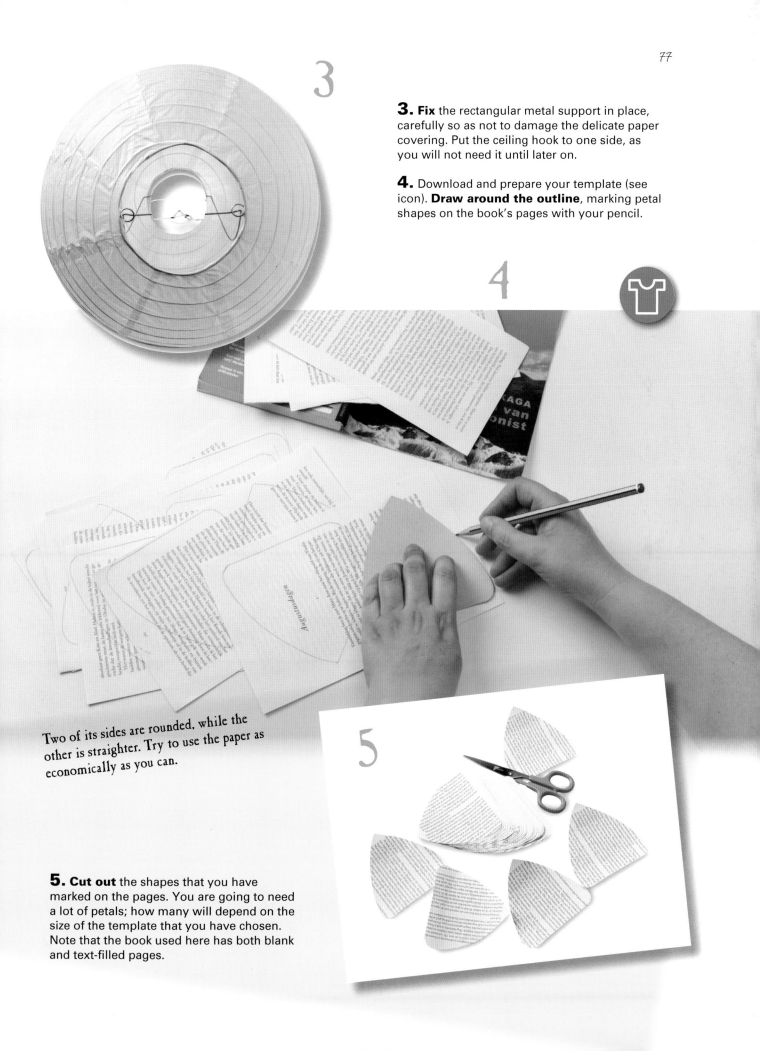

3. Fix the rectangular metal support in place, carefully so as not to damage the delicate paper covering. Put the ceiling hook to one side, as you will not need it until later on.

4. Download and prepare your template (see icon). **Draw around the outline**, marking petal shapes on the book's pages with your pencil.

Two of its sides are rounded, while the other is straighter. Try to use the paper as economically as you can.

5. Cut out the shapes that you have marked on the pages. You are going to need a lot of petals; how many will depend on the size of the template that you have chosen. Note that the book used here has both blank and text-filled pages.

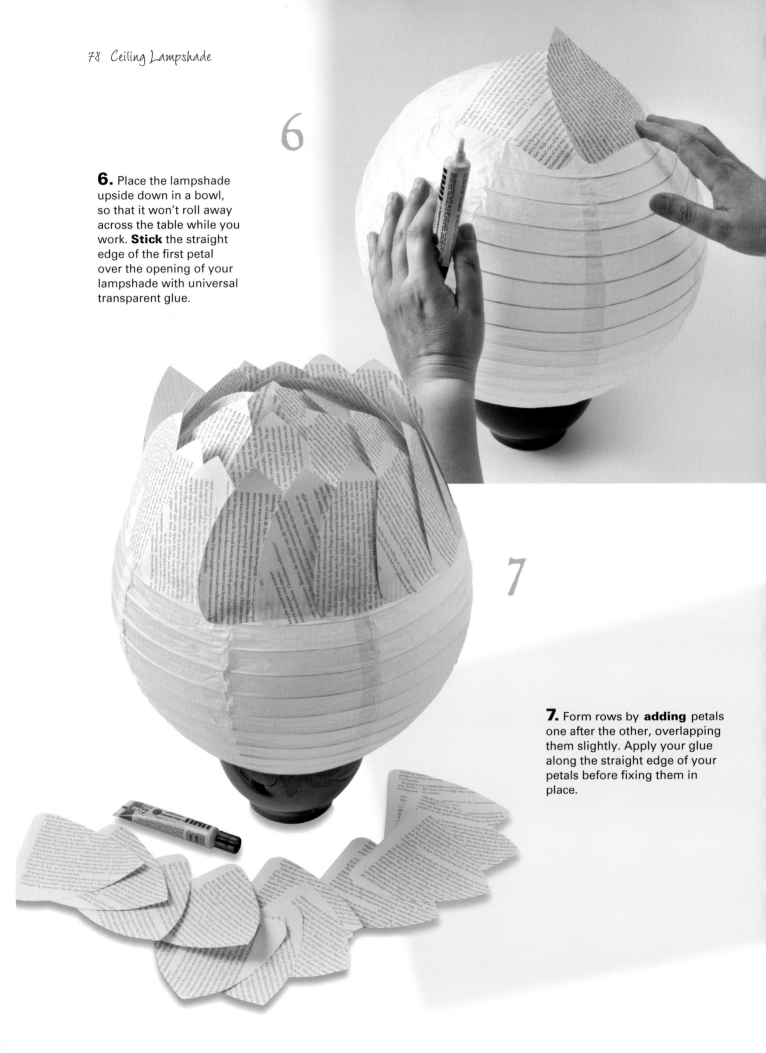

6. Place the lampshade upside down in a bowl, so that it won't roll away across the table while you work. **Stick** the straight edge of the first petal over the opening of your lampshade with universal transparent glue.

7. Form rows by **adding** petals one after the other, overlapping them slightly. Apply your glue along the straight edge of your petals before fixing them in place.

8

8. When you start a new row, make sure that you stick the first petal so that its "point" is approximately halfway between petals in the previous row, creating a flower- or fruit-like effect. The metal ribbing of the lampshade serves as an excellent guide.

This creates a flower- or fruit-like effect.

9. Cover the entire lampshade in rows of petals. You will see your project taking shape as you work!

9

10

10. As you reach the final row and stick on your last petal, make sure that it is aligned with its neighboring petals and that there are no gaps. The lampshade's substructure is now completely hidden.

Your Nordic-inspired lampshade is a striking addition to any living space, adding a touch of modern design to any room in your home.

Variations

A colorful **lampshade created from old maps** with a few too many miles on the clock is an attractive alternative. Let your imagination run free! You can plan your next vacation just by looking at it.

Using these triangles to cover a lampshade gives the impression of a flower opening its petals. **The lowest triangles give the structure a gravity-defying "floating" effect.** You may wish to reverse the direction of the rectangular metal support, allowing you to hang your lampshade upside down.

Who hasn't dreamed of having a log cabin with a birdhouse in the forest? We can at least make a birdhouse with a few unused books and use it to decorate a study, library or playroom, depending on our flight of fancy. This project allows fans of Aesop's fables and stories about fairies to daydream or fondly remember their favorite passages.

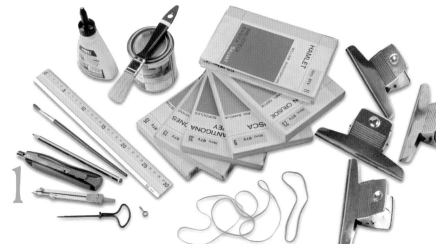

Birdhouse

1. You will need: Six unused books of equal size, PVA adhesive glue, two paintbrushes, bulldog clips, a pencil, rule, compass, scalpel, an eyebolt for hanging, a gimlet, elastic bands, and colorless sealant.

2. Carefully **remove** all six covers, as only the text blocks are required for this project.

3. Spread glue along the sides of the text blocks so that they become solid, compact blocks of paper.

4. Leave to dry, using your bulldog clips to prevent the pages from arching over.

5. Use your rule and pencil to measure and **mark out** 13/16 in. (2 cm) margins along both the bottom and top edges, and along one long edge of the text block (not the spine). This will become the base of our birdhouse.

4

5

6. Glue one of the other text blocks in place inside a margin line and on top of your base text block, forming one "wall."

6

Holding the wall in place with bulldog clips will ensure a right-angle connection to the base section.

7. Once the PVA adhesive that supports the first wall is dry, **glue** the next text block in place. Your bulldog clips should again be used to hold the structure steady.

7

8

9

10

8. Then use the PVA adhesive to **fix** the third wall of your birdhouse in place.

9. Use a compass to **trace** a circle about 2 in. (5 cm) in diameter in the middle of another text block.

10. Slowly **cut into** the text block with a scalpel, until you have made an entrance hole for your birdhouse.

You'll need to get your angles right before fashioning a perch.

11. Measure out a triangular perch that runs from the base section of your birdhouse to the entrance hole. Cut the triangle out and seal it by spreading glue around the edges.

11

12. **Stick** the perch to the front wall of your birdhouse so that birds can get a foothold.

13. **Fix** the final wall in place across the front of your birdhouse. Fasten all of the walls together with elastic bands to add stability.

14. **Punch** right through the center of the last text block with a gimlet, then fit your eyebolt ready for hanging.

15. Place the last text block on top of the structure and **glue it in place as a "roof."**

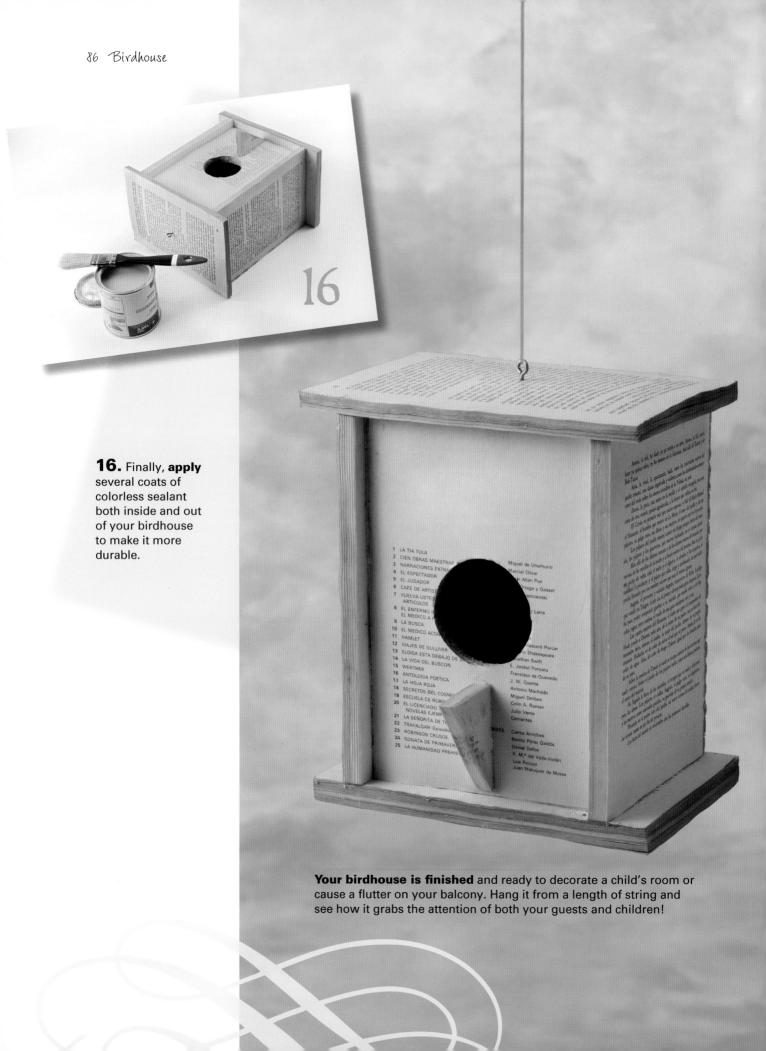

16

16. Finally, **apply** several coats of colorless sealant both inside and out of your birdhouse to make it more durable.

Your birdhouse is finished and ready to decorate a child's room or cause a flutter on your balcony. Hang it from a length of string and see how it grabs the attention of both your guests and children!

Variations

Create a fun **makeup box** with five small-format books. Simply follow the same steps as before, but this time cut gabled roof shapes into the front and rear walls. This time, leave the "roof" open.

Origami Lampshade

Origami offers us countless possibilities to recycle book pages in poor condition. By combining this folding technique with the most basic of materials you can make a captivating lampshade that will add a soft lighting effect to any corner of our homes. If you combine several different-sized lampshades you can create a "sculptural" set. This piece of Japanese-style design can also function as a vase for dried flowers.

1. You will need: Several pages from a world-weary or outdated atlas, a rule, bone paper folder, glue stick, scalpel, cutting board, and scissors.

2. Remove the white borders from an old atlas page with a scalpel, using the rule to guide you.

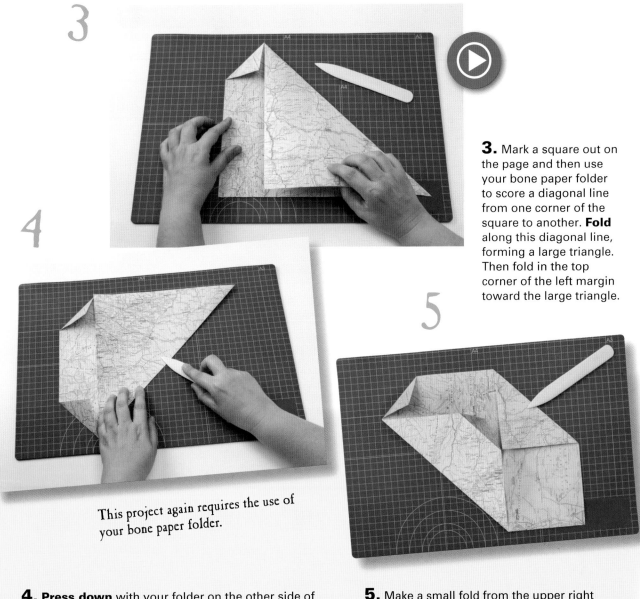

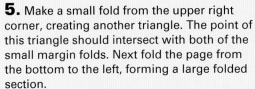

3. Mark a square out on the page and then use your bone paper folder to score a diagonal line from one corner of the square to another. **Fold** along this diagonal line, forming a large triangle. Then fold in the top corner of the left margin toward the large triangle.

This project again requires the use of your bone paper folder.

4. Press down with your folder on the other side of the long fold. Fold in the top corner of the right margin toward the large triangle.

5. Make a small fold from the upper right corner, creating another triangle. The point of this triangle should intersect with both of the small margin folds. Next fold the page from the bottom to the left, forming a large folded section.

6. Now **fold in** from opposite sides: A small fold from the lower right and a large fold from the upper left of the page. Make sure they fit snugly together.

7

7. The page is now marked with diagonal lines. **Fold** the extreme right of the page to the intersection of your previous folds, forming another small fold. Then make a large fold that matches the first fold.

8

Repeat this step from the other end of the page.

8. Make a small fold from the lower right, followed by a large fold starting from the top right.

9. Make two further folds along opposite sides of your page; firstly a large fold from the right hand side, followed by a smaller fold from the left.

9

10

11

10. Make the last two folds from opposite ends: A large fold from the lower right and a smaller fold from the top left. The edges should coincide with your previous folds.

11. Fold along the lines, **making an "accordion"** shape with the paper.

12. Cut out the resulting rhomboid shapes on either side with scissors, creating scalloped borders.

12

13

13. Form a paper cylinder, overlapping the scalloped borders and fix them together with stick glue.

All that's left to do is add a light source! Then your minimalist origami lampshade will be ready to decorate your home. You can also use this structure as a vase for dried flowers or twigs.

Variations

If you join together several **different-sized structures** made from a variety of different books, you create a striking sculptural effect.

Origami techniques offer us limitless opportunities when upcycling books. These **boxes** were made solely by folding paper, **without any need for cutting or gluing.**

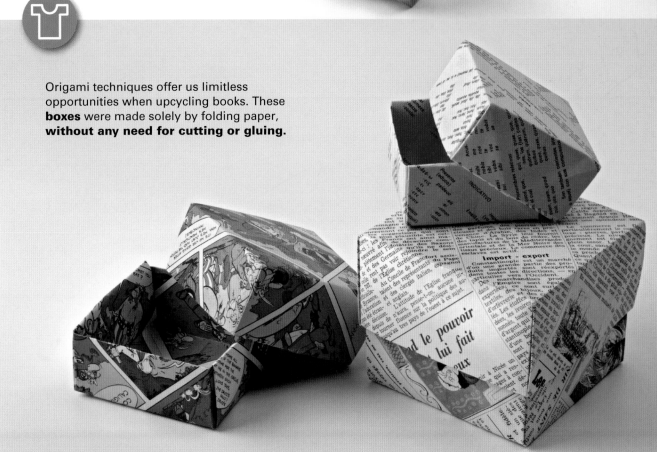

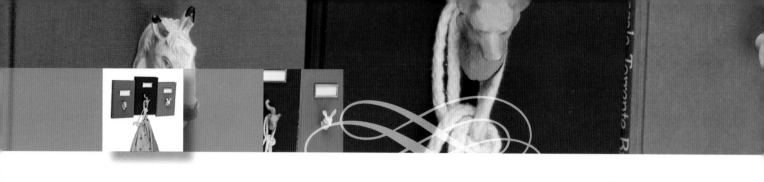

Use three old hardback books to create a simple but attractive wall hook, a decorative and practical addition to any entrance hall or child's bedroom. We have rescued some old novelty doorknobs from a local flea market, whose colors combine well with the covers of the books that we have chosen for this project. The brass label frames used here will give your wall hooks a vintage appearance, although this upcycling product can be adapted to any decorative style.

Wall Hook

1. You will need: Three unused books, three recycled or reclaimed vintage-style doorknobs, three brass label frames, a plywood board, rib saw, scalpel, gimlet, two metal wall mounts, two screws, a screwdriver, graphite pencil, white colored pencil, rule, and superglue.

2. Arrange the books on a flat surface, leaving a small gap between each book. **Place** the plywood board on top of them. Use your rule to measure the total length of your wall hook structure and mark the plywood accordingly.

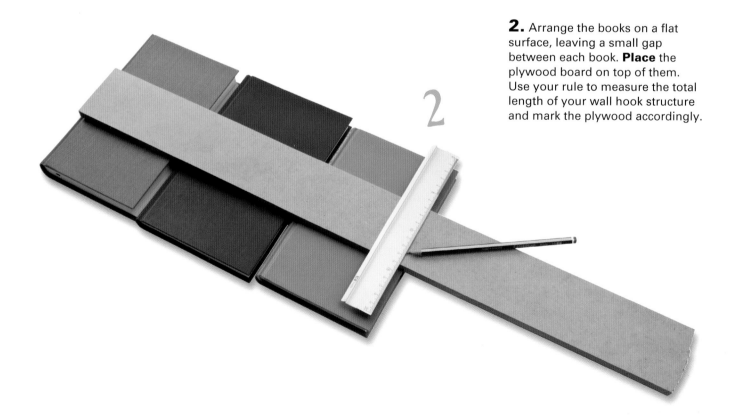

3

3. Cut into the plywood with the rib saw at the length you have measured out.

Next cut through the plywood completely.

4

4. Measure the book covers to locate the central points where you will later affix the doorknobs. **Mark** these points with your white colored pencil.

5. Place the brass label frames in place and put a mark in each of their corners.

5

6. Pierce the covers and text blocks with a gimlet (right through the books) where you will later attach your doorknobs.

7. Make slits at each of the four marks you have made for the label frames.

Use your scalpel to make the slits.

8. Then set the label frames into their slits and **fasten** them in place.

9. Insert the doorknobs into the holes that you have made in the covers, securing them with a nut and washer at the back of each book.

10. Attach the two metal wall mounts at either end of the plywood board with a screwdriver.

11

11. Place the books on your working surface and stagger them at different heights. **Apply** superglue to the plywood before sticking your books in position.

Your wall hook is ready. Its simple format makes it an ideal addition to a child's bedroom or playroom. You can personalize each hook by preparing colorful name labels for your children and slotting them into the brass frames.

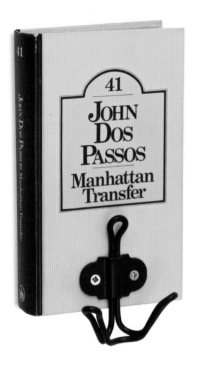

The **graphic design** of this book's cover has inspired our choice of hanger. The black frame around the text combines perfectly with the dark metallic hook.

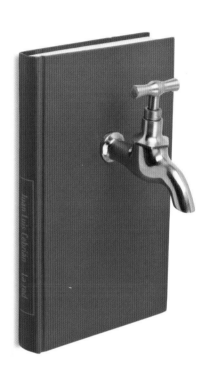

You can use **a tap** for a very different, slightly romantic effect. Our outdated book has become an original decorative piece that reminds us that literature has always been a font of insight and learning.

An unused pocket book offers many creative options if you wish to create a minimalist, **individual wall hook**. Here a doorknob has been added that contrasts with the cover colors.

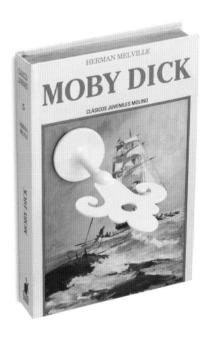

With a little imagination, a recycled **curtain rail end** and an old adventure book you can fashion a vintage-style wall hook that will inspire you to read day after day!

Retro Vase

With an old bowl you might find around the home, a balloon, an old book, and a little patience you can create a unique, strikingly designed vase. An inflated balloon allows you to form an organic structure. The technique that you will use here is so simple and the final result so spectacular that this project and its variations are wholly recommended as group work.

1. You will need: Pages from an unused book, a scalpel, cutting board, PVA adhesive glue, balloon, a bowl for your base, paintbrush, pencil, rule, and scissors.

2. Over your cutting board and with the help of a metal rule **slice** a number of long, thin paper strips with your scalpel. These strips should be ³⁄₈ in. (1 cm) wide and the entire height of the page.

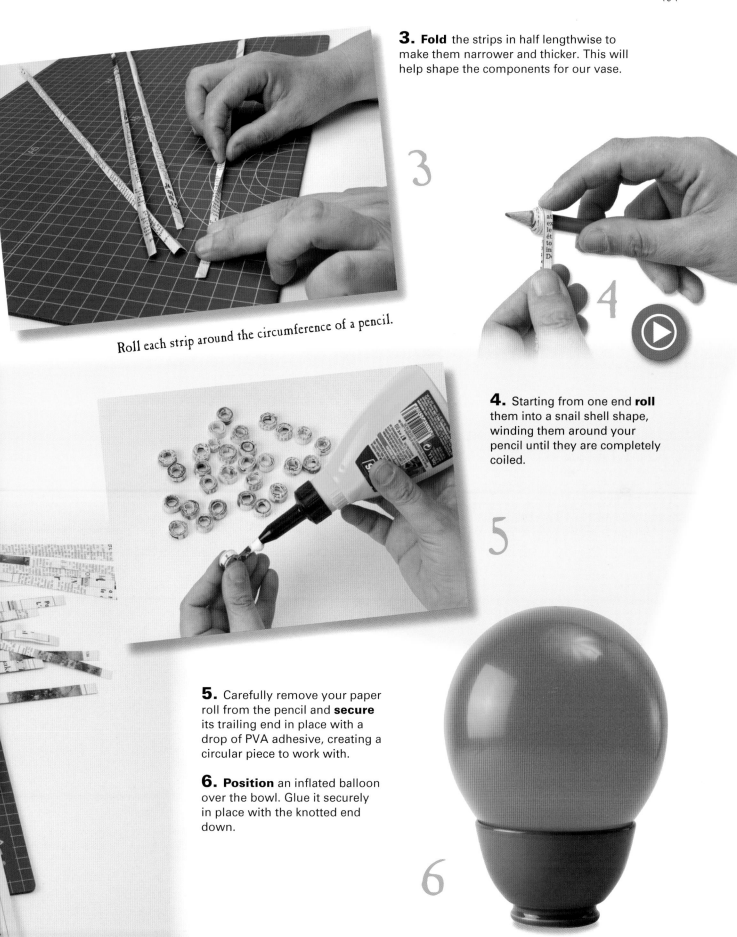

3. Fold the strips in half lengthwise to make them narrower and thicker. This will help shape the components for our vase.

Roll each strip around the circumference of a pencil.

4. Starting from one end **roll** them into a snail shell shape, winding them around your pencil until they are completely coiled.

5. Carefully remove your paper roll from the pencil and **secure** its trailing end in place with a drop of PVA adhesive, creating a circular piece to work with.

6. Position an inflated balloon over the bowl. Glue it securely in place with the knotted end down.

7. Spread PVA adhesive over the top section of the balloon.

8. Place your first paper roll at the center top point of the balloon, then begin to surround it with the other rolls.

7

Apply the paper rolls in small sections so that the glue doesn't dry while you are working.

8

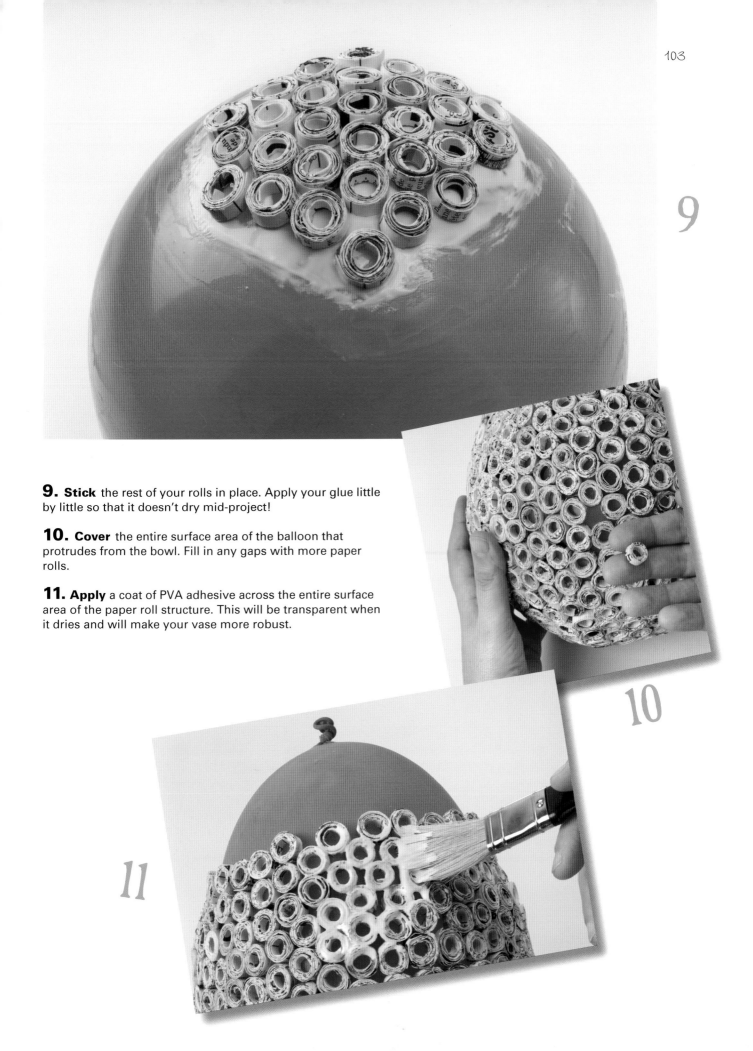

9

9. Stick the rest of your rolls in place. Apply your glue little by little so that it doesn't dry mid-project!

10. Cover the entire surface area of the balloon that protrudes from the bowl. Fill in any gaps with more paper rolls.

11. Apply a coat of PVA adhesive across the entire surface area of the paper roll structure. This will be transparent when it dries and will make your vase more robust.

10

11

12. Remove the structure from the bowl and then **pop** the balloon with one point of your scissors! Then cut away all of the balloon that is not covered by paper rolls.

12

Your retro vase is ready to brighten up any corner. You can always add a splash of color by arranging dried or silk flowers inside it.

Variations

You can use a similar technique to make a shallow basket or fruit bowl. This time you will need to select a wider-based object as the template on which to build your structure. First cover the object in plastic adhesive film and stick small **paper circles** to it. A simple technique with an elegant result!

You can use a smaller bowl as a template by layering paper **stars** created by a shaped manual punch. Stick them over a layer of plastic adhesive film and later remove the bowl.

1

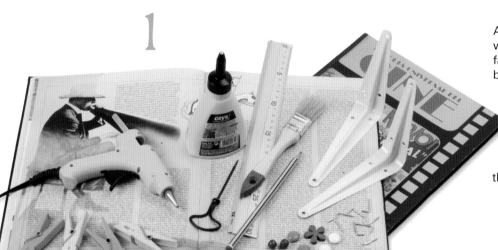

A showcase is an original, practical way to organize and store your favorite jewelry. Pendants, necklaces, bracelets, and rings are kept in plain sight, becoming decorations in themselves when the showcase is placed on a table or dresser. Furthermore, you can adapt the display format depending on the contents of the jewelry collection or the size of the book to be used.

Jewelry Showcase

1. You will need: An unused, illustrated book, pencil, rule, superglue or a hot-melt glue gun, paintbrush, PVA adhesive glue, gimlet, two shelf support brackets, stainless steel hook screws, decorative beads, and a few clothes pins.

2. Choose a compelling double-page spread that will become the backdrop of your showcase; consider its design and the composition of its text and images. Ensure that any images do not detract from the visual effect of the jewelry you will hang on it.

2

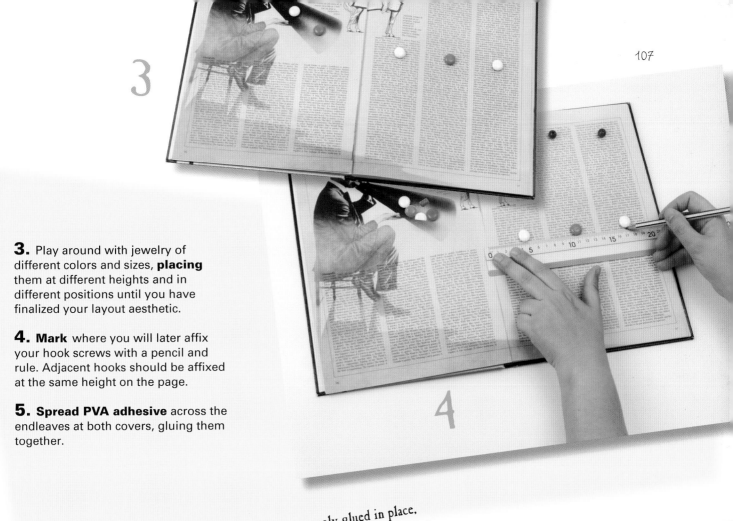

3. Play around with jewelry of different colors and sizes, **placing** them at different heights and in different positions until you have finalized your layout aesthetic.

4. Mark where you will later affix your hook screws with a pencil and rule. Adjacent hooks should be affixed at the same height on the page.

5. Spread PVA adhesive across the endleaves at both covers, gluing them together.

The endleaves and covers must be securely glued in place, so that they don't open up as you are making your showcase.

6

6. Apply more PVA adhesive along the sides of the text block and hold them in place with clothes pins while it dries.

7. Make holes with your gimlet where you have chosen to position your screw hooks.

7

8. Center one of the shelf support brackets on the back cover and fix it in place with your hot-melt glue gun.

Stand the supports on a flat surface before gluing to ensure that they are correctly positioned.

9. Place the colored beads over the ends of the screw hooks. They will act as stoppers when you hang your jewelry.

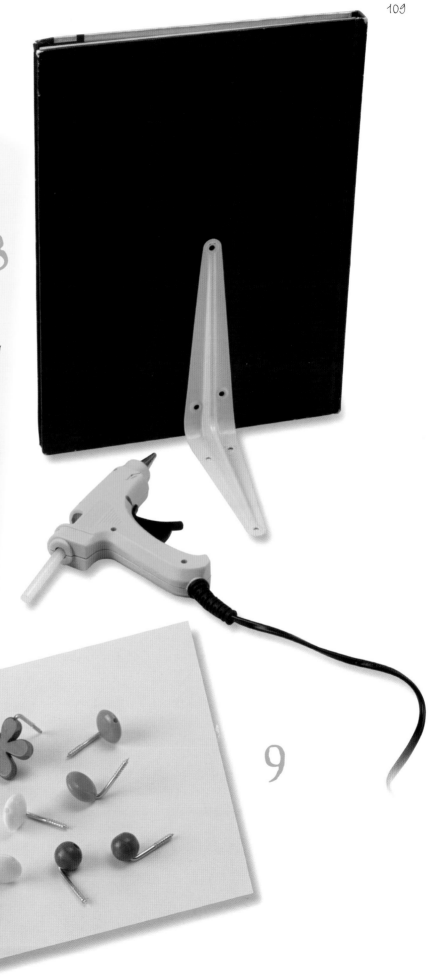

10. Position the stoppered screw hooks over the previously marked points. Carefully push them into the text block and then secure them in place by slowly turning them.

10

Your showcase is finished; all that remains to do is hang your jewelry on the hooks. The perfect way to organize your favorite necklaces and bracelets!

Variations

You can use the same technique to create a vintage-style **key holder**. In this way your keys will always be organized, kept together, and remain close at hand in case of an emergency.

You may own a large-format hardback book that is so badly damaged that you can salvage only the cover. Remember, **almost anything and everything can be recycled!** Here eyebolts have been used to hang jewelry.

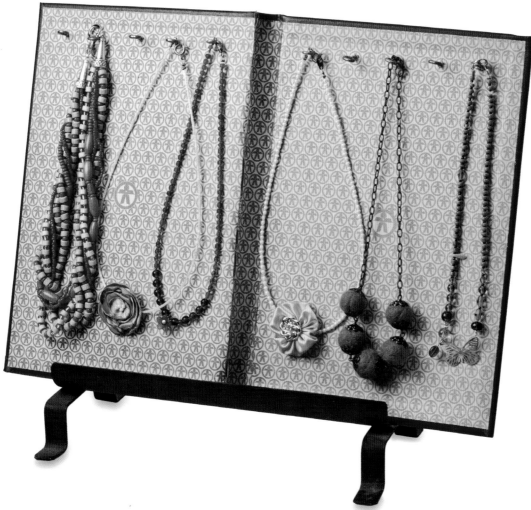

Secret Storage Box

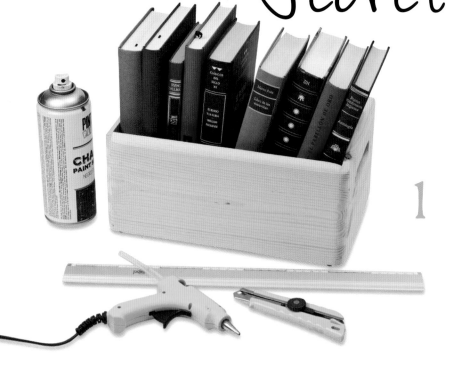

1

This project will thrill lovers of crime and mystery novels. Here you will use the spines of battered old books to create a secret storage box. It is both decorative and practical, somewhere to keep your documents, maps, letters or receipts safely hidden from view. It can be perfectly camouflaged alongside other books on a shelf, or in your library, study or office.

1. You will need: Nine unused books, a wooden box, gray aerosol (spray) paint, a rule, scalpel, and a hot-melt glue gun or mounting glue.

2. Select nine books of a similar height, which must all be taller than the sides of your wooden box. Set aside two of the books whose covers are in good condition. These will become the endpieces of your storage box.

2

3. Spray the wooden box gray with your aerosol paint.

4. Cut away the covers and text block, leaving a small margin at the spine.

Leave a small margin of text block as you cut.

3

4

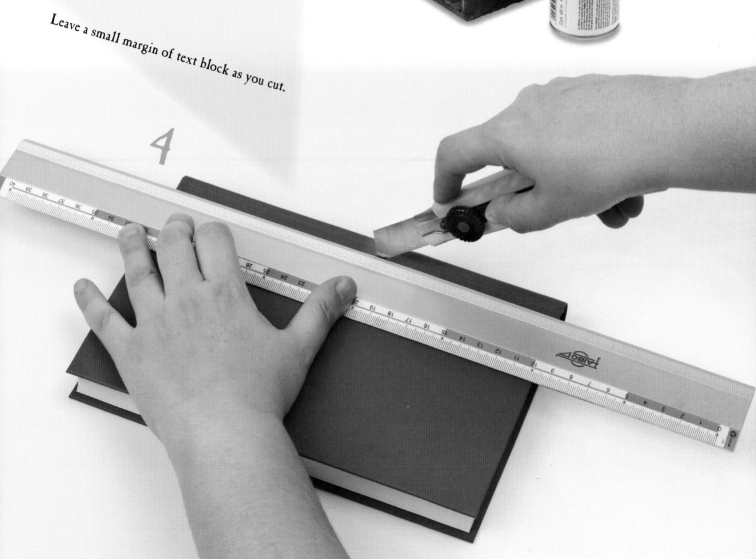

5

5. Repeat this process with six of the other books.

6. Take one of the two books that you have already set aside and carefully **cut away** the front cover and text block with a scalpel, leaving the back cover attached. Later this section will be fitted to the left-hand side of the wooden box.

6

7

7. Cut the back cover and text block away from the last book. The front cover will conceal the sides of the wooden box once you stick it in place.

8. You should be left with seven book spines, plus two more with one cover still attached.

8

9. Decide on the layout before you line the wooden box.

Set out the pieces in the order that you plan to attach them.

10. Use the hot-melt gun to **apply** silicone to one corner of the wooden box, then the inside of the textblock and cover of one of your endpiece books and stick it in place.

11. Using the spine of the first book as a guide, **secure** the next spine with silicone.

11

12. Glue the rest of the spines in place along the front of the wooden box.

12

13

13. Glue the final book (endpiece) in place. You'll need to attach both the spine and back cover.

Variations

Attaching the spines horizontally will lend your storage box a more "informal" flavor. You can also construct a **magazine rack** by lining the front and back of a bigger wooden box with larger-format books.

Your secret storage box is the ideal container for keeping small objects out of sight; it will be perfectly hidden if camouflaged among other books in your library.

A mail organizer is the perfect place to keep your correspondence tidy and organized. You can create as many pockets as books that you have available to recycle (it can also be used as a box file). Hang it in your entrance hall, where it will be useful to store written notices, bills, personal mail, and letters that you have yet to send.

1

Mail Organizer

1. You will need: Three unused books of the same size, 12 individual book pages, a wooden board, gray aerosol (spray) paint, metal wall mounts, stainless steel hook screws, white cardboard sheets, colored cardboard sheets, cutting board, sealant, a paintbrush, superglue, decorative plaques, a rule, scalpel, pencil, and white crayon.

2. Select three books of the same size to mount on your wooden board.

2

3. Cover the board with gray aerosol paint. Shake the can first and **spray on** from a distance of about 5¹⁵/₁₆ in. (15 cm).

4. Create the template with colored card, then **draw** around it onto white card before cutting it out.

You may need to apply several coats of paint to completely cover the wood.

5. Cut out six template pieces in total, two for each of your books.

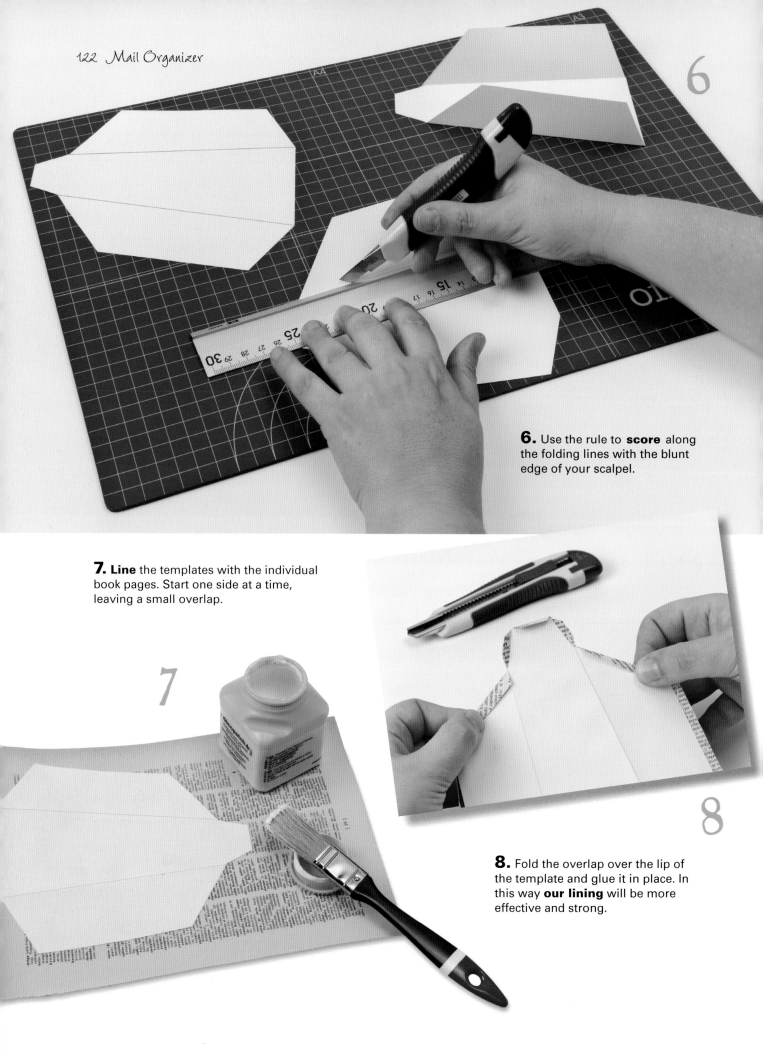

6. Use the rule to **score** along the folding lines with the blunt edge of your scalpel.

6

7. Line the templates with the individual book pages. Start one side at a time, leaving a small overlap.

7

8

8. Fold the overlap over the lip of the template and glue it in place. In this way **our lining** will be more effective and strong.

9. Apply **glue** to the other side of the templates with your paintbrush and line them with book pages too.

9

10

10. Once lined on both sides, **fold** the pieces in on themselves along the folding lines you previously scored out.

11. **Detach** the covers of all three books from their text blocks. Cutting into the inner hinges will make this job much easier.

11

12

12. Glue one of the two longer flaps to the inside spine of one of the covers, leaving a small border (about ³/₁₆ in. [0.5 cm]).

13

13. Stick the other long flap to the opposite side of the cover. You will also need two rectangular pages to line the interior of both the front and back covers, plus a thinner strip to line the spine.

14

14. Glue the remaining free edges together. **Coat** each page with sealant, which will not only make the structure more resistant to wear and tear but secure its components firmly in place.

15. Carefully **glue** a page to the inside of each pocket. The lining phase is now complete!

Fix the metal wall mounts to the top edge of the wooden board.

16

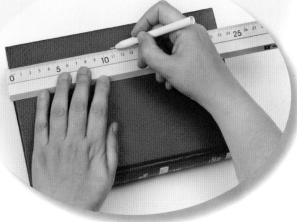

16. Use your rule to ensure that the wall mounts are equidistant from both the left- and right-hand edges of the board, to keep your organizer straight once you hang it on the wall.

17

18

17. Measure a point near to the top and dead center of each pocket, then mark it with the white crayon.

18. Then simply **glue** your decorative plaques in place over the marks.

Your mail organizer is now ready to be placed in your entrance hall or study. An incredibly useful item, it will keep all of your correspondence in order without taking up valuable surface space. Perfect for your letters and postcards!

19

19. Superglue the pockets to the wooden board, ensuring that they are straight, balanced, and evenly spaced.

Variations

With one large-format book you can make a practical yet decorative wall-mounted **magazine rack**.

If you attach some small metal feet to a pocket book's spine, you can make a petite but arresting **box for CDs, DVDs,** or other small objects.

Kitchen Utensil Holder

If your favorite recipe book has seen better days, you can give it a new lease on life by transforming it into a practical holder for storing wooden kitchen utensils. You will only need to use its covers and build in a few separators to create a brand new kitchenware accessory. Its style will vary depending on how you choose to decorate it, combine covers of different colors, and any fine detail you embellish it with.

1. You will need: Two old hardback books of different sizes, a scalpel, rule, foamboard, two different-colored corrugated cardboard sheets, glue, sealant, a paintbrush, bulldog clips, a cutting board, and two badges for decoration.

2. Use a scalpel to carefully **separate** the book covers from their text blocks.

3. Measure the height and width of the covers and the spine of the smallest book.

3

The width of the book is measured from the spine to the outside edge.

4

4. Cut four strips of foamboard to the width of the book. These will become your separators.

5

5. Line the strips by gluing yellow corrugated cardboard to them, adding a dash of color. Don't forget to line the top end of your strips too!

6. Use your rule to measure and **mark out** where you will position separators on the inside of your kitchen utensil holder.

Line the foamboard strips on both sides.

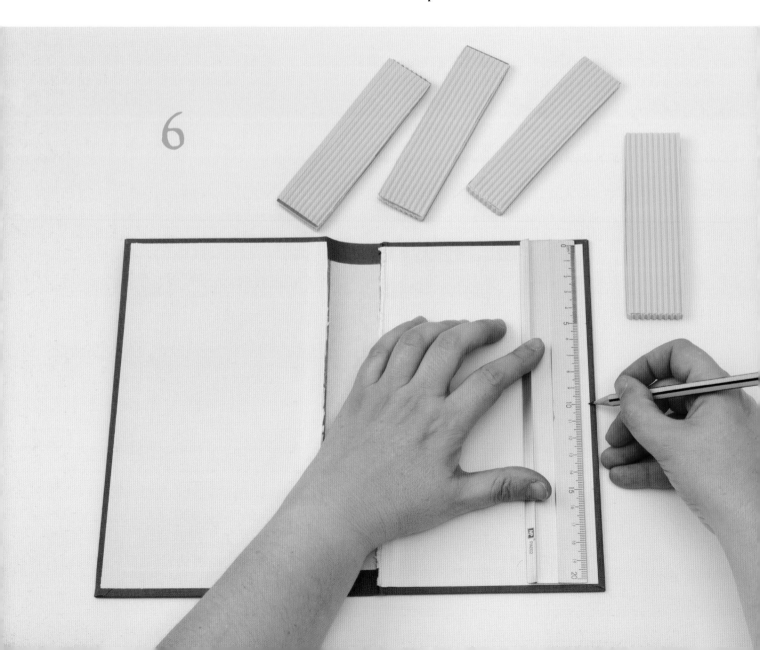

6

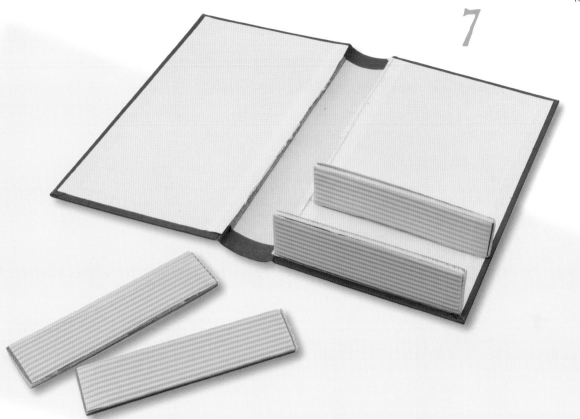

7. Glue one of the separators in place horizontally across the top of the cover.

8. Attach the remaining separators, and then glue them to the other side of the book's cover by simply closing it.

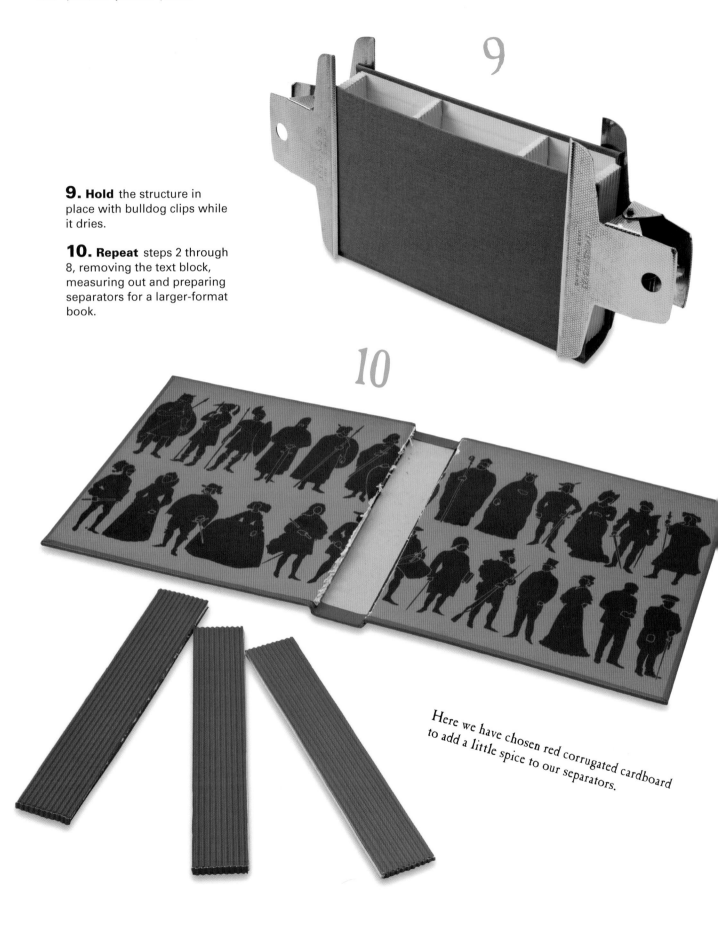

9. Hold the structure in place with bulldog clips while it dries.

10. Repeat steps 2 through 8, removing the text block, measuring out and preparing separators for a larger-format book.

Here we have chosen red corrugated cardboard to add a little spice to our separators.

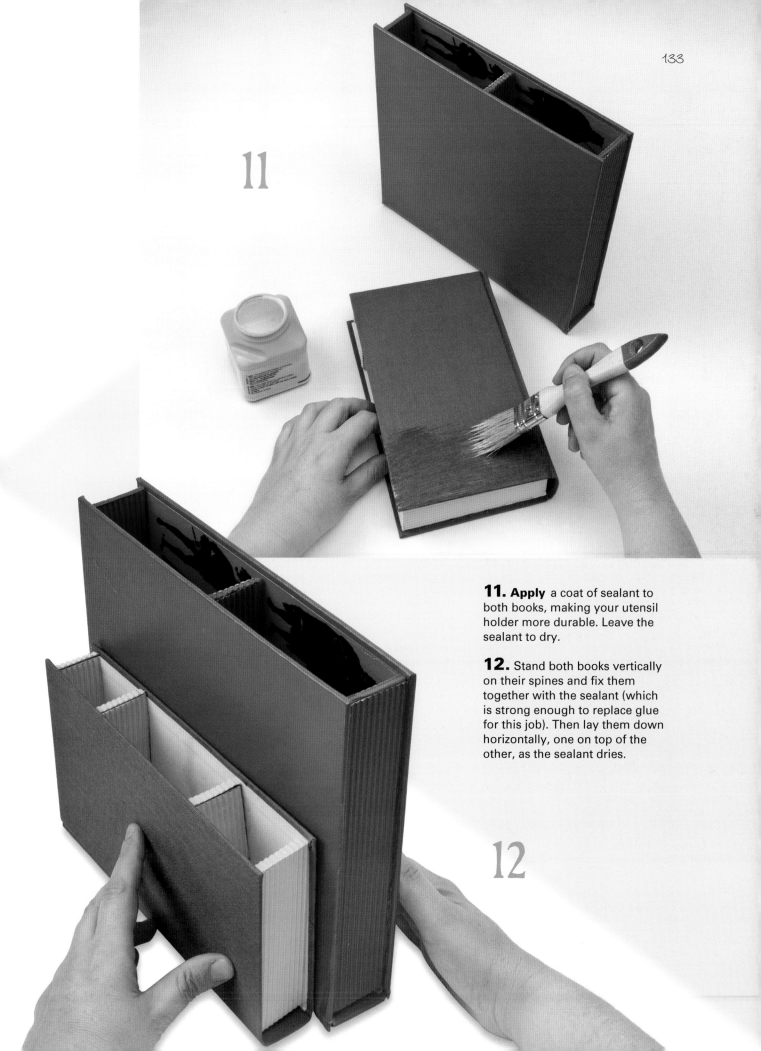

11

12. Apply a coat of sealant to both books, making your utensil holder more durable. Leave the sealant to dry.

12. Stand both books vertically on their spines and fix them together with the sealant (which is strong enough to replace glue for this job). Then lay them down horizontally, one on top of the other, as the sealant dries.

12

13. As a finishing touch, **embellish** your utensil holder with some small decorative items. Here we have chosen two dark slate badges, which contrast nicely with the brightly colored covers.

This container is ideal for keeping different kitchen utensils such as wooden spoons in order and will help you prepare any one of the recipes from your old cookbook. *Bon appétit!*

Variations

You can use the same upcycling technique to create a handy **remote organizer**, keeping your push-button devices together and close at hand.

Fairy Houses

The last project in this book is our own tribute to fairy stories, a nod to the books which so captured our imagination as children. Here you will upcycle old books to build small houses and create whole worlds to play in or simply as decoration. The important thing is to have fun and let your imagination run wild.

1. You will need: Six different-sized, unused hardback books, a scalpel, wooden board, cutting board, gray aerosol (spray) paint, a pencil, a white crayon, different-colored cardboard sheets, different-colored corrugated cardboard sheets, different-colored cocktail sticks, popsicle sticks, glue, a rule, scissors, artificial moss, a little round piece of wood, a few small figurines, and a miniature tree.

2. Use your scalpel to **separate** the books' covers from their text blocks. Draw some rectangles and squares on the spine of each book (the doors and windows of your fairy houses) in white crayon.

3. Open up the doors and windows by **cutting them out** with your scalpel.

4. Trim some cardboard rectangles on your cutting board.

Your cardboard rectangles should be the same width as the spines.

5. Line these rectangles with individual book pages and a little glue and then stick them in place, forming the "roofs" and "floors" of your fairy houses.

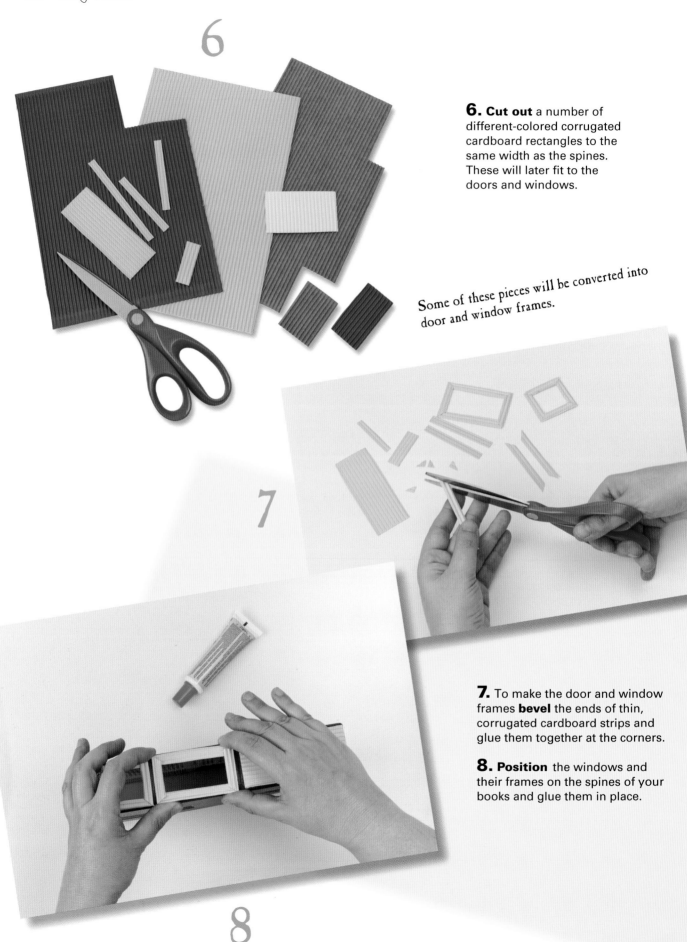

6

6. Cut out a number of different-colored corrugated cardboard rectangles to the same width as the spines. These will later fit to the doors and windows.

Some of these pieces will be converted into door and window frames.

7

7. To make the door and window frames **bevel** the ends of thin, corrugated cardboard strips and glue them together at the corners.

8. Position the windows and their frames on the spines of your books and glue them in place.

8

9. Draw grids on the back of your different-colored rectangles and squares, always remembering that these pieces must be the same width as the spine. Cut out different types of doors and windows.

10. Stick your doors in place along one side, so that they can open and close.

11. **Construct** window struts for your fairy houses from different-colored cocktail sticks.

12. **Glue** the cocktail stick window struts in place over the holes that you have cut in the spines.

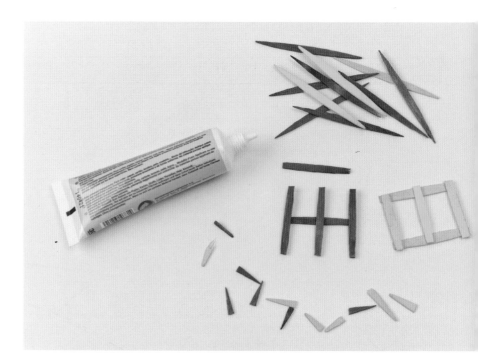

13. Take your pencil and **draw** a set of clock hands onto the little round piece of wood.

14. Then **glue** your clock to the spine of one of the books, decorating the facade.

15. Spray the wooden board gray with your aerosol paint (this is easy to apply and quickly dries).

16. Attach your books to the wooden board, leaving spaces between them to simulate alleyways.

15

16

Our fairy house tableau wouldn't be complete without a picket fence!

17

17. To build your picket fence, cut a few same-colored popsicle sticks in half and glue them in a row by running a whole popsicle stick horizontally along the bottom of the structure.

18. Glue the picket fence along the front edge of the gray wooden board and position your miniature tree. Now it's just a matter of adding the finishing touches! Scatter some artificial moss across one or more rooftops, and add a few figurines who will breathe life into the whole scene.

Fairy Street is ready for its tenants to move in! You can imagine that it is an entire city populated by a magical, miniature community that will forever feel at home inside both your book and your daydreams…

18

Variations

You can **create a room diorama** by opening a book to 90° and furnishing it with pieces from a doll's house, or even make your own accessories using any remaining pages or covers that are left over from your upcycling projects. *Let your imagination fly!*